Growing Through Setups and Letdowns

BIBLICAL BLUES

Andre Papineau

RESOURCE PUBLICATIONS, INC.
San Jose, California

Editorial director: Kenneth Guentert
Production editor: Elizabeth J. Asborno
Cover design: Ron Niewald
Cover production: Terri Ysseldyke-All
Inside illustrations: Sr. Karlyn A. Cauley, SDS

© 1989 Andre Papineau. Published exclusively by Resource Publications, Inc. All rights reserved. For reprint permission, write to the following:

Reprint Department
Resource Publications, Inc.
160 E. Virginia Street, Suite 290
San Jose, CA 95112-5848

Library of Congress Cataloging in Publication Data

Papineau, Andre, 1937-
   Biblical blues : growing through setups and letdowns / Andre Papineau.
     p.   cm.
   Includes bibliographical references.
    ISBN 0-89390-157-1
   1. Spiritual life—Catholic authors.   I. Title.
BX2350.2.P295   1989
248.4—dc20   89-37532

5 4 3 2 1

93 92 91 90 89

Scripture selections taken from the **New American Bible** *Copyright © 1970 by the Confraternity of Christian Doctrine, Washington, D.C., are all used with permission of copyright owner. All rights reserved.*

CONTENTS

Acknowledgments vi
Introduction: Setups and Letdowns 2

SETUPS

MINE 24
PORCELAIN PROBLEM 30
EXTRAVAGANCE 36
Reflection: *I'm really somebody
because of what I own* 42

POWER PLAY 44
Reflection: *I'm really somebody
because of my position* 50

THE COMPANY 52
Reflection: *I'm really somebody
because of the company I keep* 58

TRIPPED UP 60
THE KINGDOM 68
FAR RIGHT 74
Reflection: *I'm really somebody
because I have a corner on salvation* 81

WHERE ARE YOU? 84
Reflection: *I'm really somebody
because I talk a good game* 91

JUDAS 92
Reflection: *I'm really somebody
because you're my everything* 99

PIG-HEADED 102
Reflection: *I'm really somebody
because I'm always right* 109

SUPERSTAR 110
Reflection: *I'm really somebody
because I'm number one* 117

JOE'S BOY 118
Reflection: *I'm really somebody
because we're in the know* 124

SPECIAL 126
Reflection: What Makes Us Special? 134

LETDOWNS

PARANOID 138
Reflection: *Deep down I'm nobody
because everybody let me down* 144

SAM: A HERO IN SPITE OF HIMSELF . . . 146
Reflection: *Deep down I'm nobody
because it's a dog-eat-dog world* 152

LAZARUS 154
Reflection: *Deep down I'm nobody
because my body let me down* 160

LITTLE MAN	162
BETTER OFF	168
Reflection: *Deep down I'm nobody because I let myself down*	173
BECOMING A MAN	176
Reflection: *Deep down I'm nobody because you died and let me down*	182
ORDERS	184
Reflection: *Deep down I'm nobody because something in me died since you left*	190
SIMEON	192
Reflection: *Deep down I'm nobody because my children left me*	197
PETER'S UNFINISHED BUSINESS	200
Reflection: *Deep down I'm nobody because my friend let me down*	206
UP AND DOWN	210
Reflection: *Deep down I'm nobody because my work is gone*	215
THE LAST REQUEST	218
Reflection: A Disillusioned God?	225
Bibliography	228

Acknowledgments

In the summer of 1988, while I lived at St. Malachy's (the Actors' Chapel in New York City), I wrote most of the stories in this volume. I would like to dedicate this book to all of my friends at St. Malachy's, who have been so gracious to me since my first summer visit in 1980. During subsequent visits, particularly during my sabbatical, I have always felt at home. St. Malachy's has a special place in my heart because it was on the feast of the Epiphany, 1984, that I gave my first story, "The Vision." The marvelous reception accorded the story provided me the motivation and the inspiration to continue writing stories since that time.

My special thanks to Dan Pekarske, SDS, for the innumerable hours he has spent editing the material in my books. Without his help and encouragement, I never would have entertained the idea of publishing at all.

BIBLICAL BLUES

Introduction: Setups and Letdowns

"I've been set up!"
"I've been let down!"
We hear these expressions over and over. Whether someone has actually set us up or let us down isn't the issue. What is important is our *perception* of being forever set up or let down. The stories in this volume are about the innumerable setups and letdowns that we experience over a lifetime. It will be worthwhile to explore in detail not only what we mean by these setups and letdowns but also the crucial role they play in our psychological and spiritual development. At times the journey toward understanding may be rough going because of the territory we are exploring. But the stories will help us understand the introduction more clearly, just as the introduction will aid us in appreciating the stories.

Introduction: Setups and Letdowns

Setups

The setup can be understood actively and passively. Ordinarily we speak of *being* set up. Expressions like *taken in, suckered, caught up, seduced, tricked, conned, captivated,* and *enchanted* reflect this passive view of the setup. We get *caught up* with our work, for example. Or we are *taken in* by a fast talking salesperson; *taken for a ride* by a con artist. A powerful personality mesmerizes and seduces us into doing what we would not normally do.

Less obvious, and so more subtle, is our active contribution to the setup. Without being conscious of it, we engage in a quasi-conspiracy with the forces setting us up. Idols fascinate and hold our attention, but only because at some level we yearn to give ourselves over to someone or something. We may act coy, cute, or seductive toward the person who is leading us on. Sometimes we go looking for trouble and when we find it, we accuse someone else of setting us up. A Japanese adage expresses the active-passive nature of the setup: "First the man takes a drink. Then the drink takes a drink. Then the drink takes the man."

Our willingness to be set up can be explained only by understanding how a person, place, or thing can satisfy our need for meaning. The object of our fascination is something that can center us and give direction to our lives. Think of a man who has fallen in love and how he yearns for nothing else but to be with the woman of his dreams. Wherever he goes, whatever he does, and whomever he sees all become occasions for celebrating her. Think, too, of addicts and how the object of addiction dominates their lives. The "fix" can be food, alcohol, drugs, sex, work, etc. Whatever it is,

Introduction: Setups and Letdowns

it is crucial to their existence. Without it, they fall apart; with it, their lives seem to hold together—at least for a while. Yet, sooner or later the bubble bursts and the setup turns into a letdown.

Letdowns

If we had been led to believe parents are perfect, we learn one day that dad cheats on his income tax. Or if we marry and think our partner the ideal mate, we discover she or he isn't all that perfect. "Well I thought at least you'd understand," we complain bitterly to an uncomprehending partner. We grow up with the notion that the church is holy mother and become disillusioned sooner or later as we realize she is also a whore. Life holds promise at eighteen, but at mid-life seems empty and flat. Finally, when we retire, we are given a gold pen, a chicken dinner, and a send-off to Retirement Park Village where we are bored silly. We are disenchanted; we've been had. As a result we feel betrayed and get depressed.

Betrayal is like jumping from the top of the stairs, expecting someone we trust will be at the bottom to catch us—and no one's there. We end up broken and bleeding. To feel betrayed is to feel abandoned, dumped, used. Several years ago James Hillman wrote an insightful essay on betrayal. In it he catalogued the various reactions a betrayed person may have toward the perceived betrayer. If we bring to mind the big letdowns we have experienced in life, we will probably recognize these reactions: revenge, denial, cynicism, self-rejection, and paranoia.

Introduction: Setups and Letdowns

Revenge is wanting to get even with and destroy the other—wanting to hurt someone as deeply as we have felt hurt. An eye for an eye; a tooth for a tooth. While it is a normal reaction, our desire for revenge can become so obsessive that we injure ourselves in the effort to get even with the enemy.

Another reaction is **denial**. If in our setups we idolize, angelize, and idealize the object of our fascination, in the letdown we demonize it. What we formerly had regarded as ideal we now consider irredeemably flawed. Whereas in the setup the other could do no wrong, now wrong is all the other *can* do.

Cynicism is yet another common reaction to betrayal. Having gotten burned in one situation, cynics generalize that all similar situations will lead to similar results. For example, if a man has cheated on a woman, then she may conclude all men are cheats. Or if one bishop is found out to be a liar, then they are all liars. And if one politician is corrupt, they all must be. The cynic's response to betrayal is never to trust again. Having been deeply hurt, they believe trusting again will simply lead to more pain. Consequently, cynicism becomes a defensive ploy to prevent further hurt.

Potentially, one of the most destructive reactions to betrayal is **self-betrayal.** It is one thing to feel rejected by someone; it is quite another to reject ourselves. In self-rejection we deny some important aspect of ourselves: usually that facet of ourselves wherein we had been most open and vulnerable to the one who has betrayed us. Self-rejection, like cynicism, is a defense mechanism. If being tender has led to suffering, we are determined never to be tender again. Or if our truthfulness has caused rejection, we promise ourselves never to tell another what we honestly think. Unfortunately our wounds are never healed solely by anesthetizing ourselves to pain.

Hillman's advice to us is *not* to disavow the vulnerable aspects of ourselves that have allowed us to feel hurt, but to own those parts of ourselves. For it is precisely there that we have revealed and perhaps discovered for the first time what is most genuine and real in ourselves. The conscious affirmation, "But this is me and I will not deny it," is painful but also life-affirming. On the other hand, disavowal is equivalent to burying what is distinctive to the person.

Finally, we may become **paranoid** in our reaction to betrayal. The betrayed person demands that everyone in all future relationships will promise in blood never to betray us. Trust is no longer the issue since the paranoid believes that the only sound basis for a relationship must be one of power and control.

Depression

If the sense of betrayal figures prominently in the aftermath of a letdown, so too does depression. We often speak of feeling down, of being in the dumps, of having the blahs and the blues. Perhaps the severity of the mood connected with the letdown depends on how acutely we experience our losses. That in turn may be determined by how closely what is lost had been identified with our sense of self. If a woman, for example, has identified her husband's future with her own, and if she has attempted to derive her satisfaction entirely through pleasing him, then she may become very depressed during their marriage or after a divorce. The setup in this situation is that her

Introduction: Setups and Letdowns

husband had been expected to provide meaning and fulfillment for her, while the letdown is the realization that this is a pipe dream, an illusion.

Depression does not distort reality; in fact, it is the mood wherein the truth first comes to light. Lesley Hazleton challenges the idea that the depressed person has a distorted understanding of reality. She maintains that the onset of depression follows from seeing through illusions and myths that supplied false security and shielded us from the harshness of reality. Without oversimplifying the complex issue of the origins of depression, clearly being depressed can mean seeing things as they are and not through the distorted lens of illusion.

If it is true that depression leads to or flows from having outgrown a certain illusion, can the "dark" demon of depression actually bear a message of light and liberation? In her excellent survey of theories on depression, Janice Wetzel prefers to view depression as an internal barometer indicating that the maturation process is either being retarded or forced too quickly. From this point of view, depression is not a disease or something alien to the organism. Depression need not be pathological. It can be liberating insofar as it signals something that impedes or rushes growth. That "something" is often an illusion, a set of assumptions, for example, about how we are to live our lives or what is supposed to happen to nice people like us.

The Self

Later we shall consider how we can understand the potentially creative role of depression in interpersonal

Introduction: Setups and Letdowns

relationships with others and with God. However, at this point it will be worthwhile to reflect on the positive contribution of setups and letdowns by describing how the psychiatrist Carl Jung thought we experienced our core or central reality, which he called the Self. Originally we are unconscious of the Self and first experience its different dimensions through projections—that is, we first become aware of ourselves as we see ourselves in others. For example, we find ourselves attracted or repelled by someone who seems to have the power to center us or captivate our interest. Jung maintained that such attraction takes place only partially because of the qualities the other person possesses. The other ingredient in this enchantment is our own as yet undiscovered Self or center that we have unconsciously projected onto the other. Thus, in and through the other person, we experience our own hidden depths, both its positive and the negative dimensions.

We are irritated or repelled by some people not only because of negative qualities they possess (which we often greatly exaggerate), but also because they evoke what is negative in us. Often these are things that we cannot admit about ourselves and can only project unconsciously onto others. Similarly, qualities we deeply admire in others can be a shadow of similar good qualities hidden in ourselves that we likewise project onto others. Infatuation is a good illustration of the cycle of setup and letdown, in which we project first positive and then negative qualities of ourselves onto another. Only when we realize what we're doing and withdraw all of our projections can we finally own those heretofore hidden dimensions of ourselves.

When we are infatuated, we see only what is most admirable, loving, and beautiful in another, as in an

Introduction: Setups and Letdowns

idol. The other becomes a bearer of existing qualities we are blind to in ourselves. We cannot see or permit ourselves to see the other apart from our positive projections. We want to maintain the illusion that the other is perfect, and we need to repress the other's negative qualities, what Jung called the shadowy, dark side of the person. Others are more likely to see flaws in the person we idolize and they might even try to point out the other's limitations. However, we may actually regard those limitations as enhancing the other's desirability, not detracting from it. A smile, nervous laugh, or manner of speech which irritates someone else is adorable, cute, and wonderful to us. The other can do no wrong! For he or she is the bearer of the Self, and we have fallen in love with ourselves in the other.

The setup is the collusion of our need to idolize and of the other's willingness for the time being to be that idol. Initially the other may be delighted at getting so much attention and may even attempt to be everything we need. However, in time the other feels put upon and has no breathing space to be him or herself. He or she feels like a statue or an object, not a person. From a developmental point of view, if the relationship is to move beyond this stage, a change has to occur. To appropriate what we have projected, a letdown is essential.

Painfully, we become aware the other isn't god; the person's limitations begin to dawn. Ever more desperately, we prop up the idol as the awareness grows that it is an idol *we* have constructed. We make excuses, rationalize, and attempt to justify the other's behavior. We get angry and feel hurt, but we're eager to forgive and forget if only we can maintain the illusion. Why? Because this is the only way in which

Introduction: Setups and Letdowns

we have been able to experience hitherto unknown positive dimensions of the Self. The other has brought to life something within that is precious (e.g., a reflective or humorous side), and we fear the death of the relationship may mean that what has come to life in ourselves might also die. The degree to which the other captivates, enchants, and psychologically holds us in bondage and we in turn are willing to lose our Self in the other suggests how difficult or easy it will be to regain our independence as a separate self.

But however painful, only a full-scale letdown presents us the opportunity to be liberated from making another person the center around which our lives revolve. It is also an invitation to relate consciously to those qualities of ours that we have given allegiance to as though they belonged to another.

Jung's point is that we need to consciously own what is most real in us, our Self, and that we do this only by projecting dimensions of our Self onto others, idolizing ourselves in others and then withdrawing those projections. If this is so, if there is a positive side to this painful cycle of idolization/demonization/acceptance, then perhaps some of our reactions to betrayal also contain something of value. But how can denial and cynicism make a positive contribution?

Setups and Letdowns As Positive Experience

In denial, the tendency to regard the other as a demon may be the necessary initial step in gaining a sense of our own separateness. If we have relied too

Introduction: Setups and Letdowns

excessively on others, been too dependent on them for our sense of self, and if we have defined who we are solely on the basis of our relationship with another, then we may have to experience the other as someone mean and devious in order to separate psychologically. Only then can we appropriate our center, which we had unconsciously handed over to and discovered only in the other. We may have first to denounce, deny, and denigrate someone whom we had admired so much because we are still very attached to and dependent on that person. We make all kinds of negative projections in order to regain the Self we had invested in the other. Our own Self-interest is at stake, and if we view interest as energy, then the other, as bearer of energy, has to be symbolically slain (let down) if we are to regain that energy. Adolescents sometimes need to see their parents as ogres because their reliance on the All-Provident may prevent them from striking out on their own and discovering they too are potentially bearers of the power of the All-Provident.

Of course this denial or depreciation of the other ought to move to a new phase: seeing that what we denied was not only the other's limitations, imperfections, peccadilloes, and idiosyncrasies, but our own shadow or negative side in the other. We have to recognize how we have demonized the other with our own demons: that what we don't like in them is amplified by our own negative traits. In this process we want to move *from* idolizing *through* demonizing *to* humanizing so that we can finally recognize people as they are, no more no less, people with their limitations even as we have ours. Disenchantment, the letdown, moves us through a process of owning positive

Introduction: Setups and Letdowns

projections, projecting negative ones, and owning them—all for the sake of coming to fuller consciousness of who we are.

The cynicism in disenchantment may likewise have a positive contribution. Cynics not only see through their previous overvaluations of a person, place, institution, etc., but they tend to generalize their new undervaluations about every person, place, etc. In other words, cynics undervalue or deflate most everything. Nothing is worthwhile. Nobody is all that good. Everything is phony and unreal. Whatever others hold valuable, cynics perceive to be sham or questionable. The positive side of this negative attitude is the discovery that nothing or nobody *is* god, and the cynic testifies to this truth out of this mood. Of course the danger is that cynicism as a permanent mood or state leads to despair, the despair of any meaning, ever. A creative cynic, on the other hand, sees God by denying the reality of God in any and every idol made to look like God. "Vanity of vanities and all is vanity," is the response of the truly religious person, who like the cynic, sees through illusions.

Setups and Letdowns
As Religious Experience

We have considered certain insights from psychology that help us understand the necessity of setups and letdowns for the development and maintenance of the person. What we have not addressed, however, is the specifically religious dimension of setups and letdowns. Viewing enchantment and disenchantment

Introduction: Setups and Letdowns

within the context of the religious quest yields interesting results. Sam Gill, in an extremely perceptive article on certain religious rites of passage among preliterate tribal societies, has shown that the goal of spiritual transformation in the novices is accomplished through a series of ceremonies corresponding to what I have been calling setups and letdowns. For example, in one initiation ceremony, the elders of the community dress up as the tribal deities and present themselves as such to the wide-eyed novices. Then in another ceremony, although the elders again come disguised as the gods, they later reveal themselves not to be gods at all but the tribal elders. There is a sense of betrayal among the novices because they realize they have been duped by the elders.

Why are the novices encouraged to believe the gods are among them and then disabused of that very belief? According to Gill, there is an important pedagogical value in this. First, the novices are given the opportunity to experience the gods concretely and visibly in the masked elders parading as gods. We might label this approach to experiencing the holy as 'sacramental'. That which is invisible, the holy, becomes tangible and available in space and time via the masked elders.

However, later the novices are discouraged from simply *identifying* the masked figures with the deities. The young initiates are forced to realize that while the invisible becomes apparent in the visible, the invisible is always more than any of its concrete manifestations. In other words, the novices must arrive at a more sophisticated appreciation of the holy and embrace the tension that the holy is here in this object, place, and thing, but that it exists beyond any concrete appearances.

Introduction: Setups and Letdowns

How does our consideration of setups and letdowns in rites of passage provide a religious context for understanding our own experiences? Perhaps we can describe our own desire to be fulfilled as a desire to be totally united with Totality, Being, God, etc., without our necessarily being consciously aware this is what we are seeking. And in our passionate drive toward this union, time and again we light on this person or that thing with the unspoken assumption: "This is it! This is what I am looking for!" Not realizing it, we are setting ourselves up! We are expecting to find our total fulfillment in this or that limited reality. Letdown is inevitable when we discover the concrete other is not and can never be the all in All. Again, we might not use religious language to describe our disillusionment, but the truth is we really had looked to the other as to one who could fulfill our deepest aspirations. Just as the elders revealed themselves as mere mortals in the rites of passage, so the people, places, things, and institutions whom we idolize have to be revealed as vehicles of the divine but never, never the divine itself.

Our letdowns, our sense of betrayal, instruct us, as they did the novices, that what we identified as god is very limited, very fragile, very human. Yet the setup and the letdown have drawn us outside of ourselves both to search for the truly holy and to reject whatever passes for the divine but isn't. The search for the holy is an ongoing search in which we reach for the holy and grasp what will always be limited. The setup is the temporary illusion that we have in fact grasped the holy, and the letdown is the painful realization that the holy necessarily eludes our grasp and comprehension.

Addiction

It is within the context of a religious search with its setups and letdowns that we might profitably reflect on the meaning of addiction. Unfortunately we tend to focus on the addictive personality as sick or maladjusted. Whatever merit there is in this assessment is lost if we do not consider addiction as fundamentally a religious problem. Based on the preceding discussion, we could say the addict wants to surrender to the object of the addiction as the absolute fulfillment of the addict's being. The addict is in search of meaning, as we all are. But as Van Kaam has remarked, the addict wants fulfillment with the least possible responsibility, mastery, decision, or commitment—that is, without actively being a responsive and responsible member of society.

The addict seeks the holy without regard for living an embodied existence in which the tasks of daily living must be carried out. He or she surrenders totally or lives an exclusively receptive mode of existence in the addiction. In other words, the setup, the addiction, claims the addict's allegiance in much the same way the worshiper is drawn toward the holy. However, there is an important difference between addiction and authentic worship. The addict gets hooked, absorbed, and captivated by a limited manifestation of the holy (e.g., romantic love, drugs, alcohol, religious rituals, etc.), whereas the genuine worshiper is capable of appreciating the limited manifestation without equating the appearance with the holy. Thus, as much as authentic worship involves a reverence and respect for rituals, dogmas, creeds, religious leaders, or created goods, these realities are not idolized and

Introduction: Setups and Letdowns

made to be the divine. The worshiper is able to experience the holy in a variety of ways, whereas the addict is caught up with a limited, partial disclosure and cannot move beyond that.

Understanding addiction as originating in the search for the holy or for meaning doesn't negate the psychological considerations of setups and letdowns offered earlier. Rather, it affords a more comprehensive approach to understanding this phenomenon. So, too, our understanding of depression can be enriched if we view it within a religious context. For this we can draw on the time- honored concept within the Christian tradition: the dark night.

Bypassing Impasses

Constance Fitzgerald, in her article "Impasse and Dark Night," has capably pointed out that the dark night in human relationships is the result of the withdrawal of our projections: when we come to see others as they are apart from the distorting effects of our needs. Stripped of our customary ways of seeing another, we are at a *loss* as to how to relate. We experience no consolation or satisfaction in the relationship and we don't know which way to turn. We are at an impasse, dead-ended and depressed. We are tempted to give up altogether, but it is precisely at this impasse that we may be on the verge of breakthrough.

Impasse in this context means reason fails us and we cannot "figure" a way out. No one and nothing is capable of helping us, and we feel abandoned and alone. All we can do is admit our complete helplessness and surrender our desire to control the outcome, while

Introduction: Setups and Letdowns

waiting for deeper unconscious processes to move us toward a creative resolution. What transpires on that level we might designate *a movement of the Self,* although Fitzgerald doesn't use this term. Our usual ego-centered approach, our ordinary way of thinking and acting in this situation, no longer works, and we submit to the movement of the Self, hoping for some guidance.

To understand this impasse, this inability on one level to do anything, and the breakthrough that can occur on another level, we need only reflect on our own lives. We are in the dark and we don't know which way to turn. Unable to decide anything, we cry out in our helplessness and we wonder if we will ever find an answer. Imperceptibly, however, we begin to discover a decision *has been* made. We have already made up our minds in a strange, mysterious way. Someone or something has been at work within us.

During an impasse we are often depressed. Stripped of the comforting illusions about who we are and who the other is, we feel empty and arid, not to mention guilty since we feel "bad" about our failure in the relationship. But however depressed we may feel, disillusionment is a purifying process during which we see through the nexus of projections that have inhibited us from developing a more mature, deeper love. This is the intimate connection between disenchantment and depression.

Fitzgerald applies this interpersonal understanding of impasse to our relationship to God. Not surprisingly, we relate to God through a network of projections that reflect our particular needs to see God in a certain way. We construct God in our own image and likeness. But at a certain point in the relationship, the projections fail. They have to be withdrawn if we are to relate

17

Introduction: Setups and Letdowns

to God in any satisfying way. But for a while, we are left at an impasse. Who is God? What is God? With the death of our illusions, we are at a loss. It is the dark night when, suffering the loss of illusion, we seem to have lost everything. We are empty, dried up. We are depressed. It is during the dark night that our way of praying and approaching God no longer works and, as in our other interpersonal dealings, we confess our inability to "manage" our relationship with God. We submit ourselves to the Mystery by waiting quietly in the dark as the Mystery purifies us of our illusions and we arrive at an even more profound experience of this Mystery.

We can summarize what we have considered about setups and letdowns by reflecting on the diagram on the following page. On the left end of the line is the Self and on the right the Other. What we would expect between adults would be a simple act of regard, a simple act of seeing. "Hi, this is me," and "So that's you" illustrated in the broken line. But as we have just seen, things are never so simple. Unable to accept ourselves fully, we project. During the phase of enchantment, we project our needs, idealizations, expectations, and assumptions onto the Other until, at the top of the curve, we have made of the Other an idol (i.e., overvalued, angelized, etc.). But the Other cannot bear our projections indefinitely. During the phase of disenchantment, we withdraw positive projections. As the curve moves downward, it plummets below the line of normal seeing and the Other becomes the target of our negative projections. Here we demonize or undervalue the Other. The entire decline is also a depressing time because we are suffering from loss, the loss of illusion. Finally, in the best scenario, the curve gradually moves upward to meet the Other on the line. This

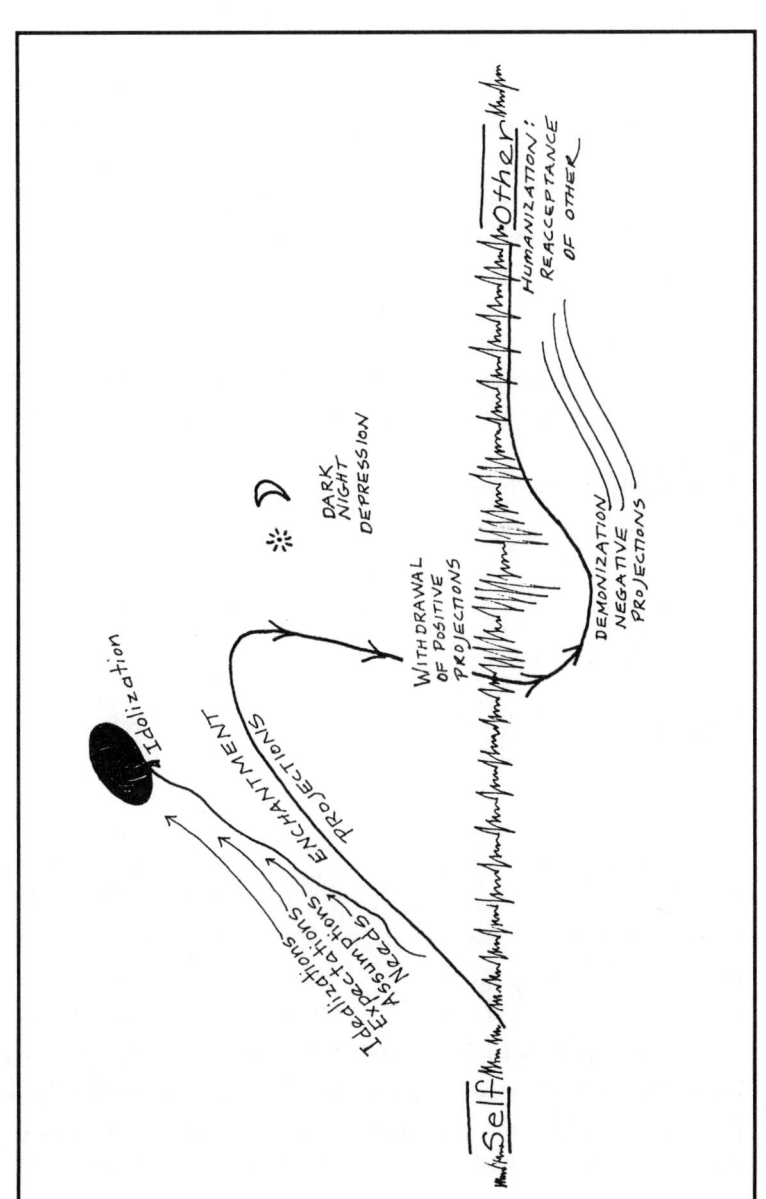

Diagram: Projections

Introduction: Setups and Letdowns

is the humanizing phase, during which we reappropriate ourselves and reaccept the Other. It is the time of withdrawing negative projections and seeing the other as he or she is, not as a saint or a sinner but as saint/sinner, as a human being. Equally important, we accept ourselves as saint/sinner, as fully human. We see and accept ourselves and one another on an equal basis. We might think of the setup as heaven (albeit false), the letdown as hell, and the new relationship as resurrection.

About This Book

The Stories

The stories that follow illustrate various aspects of setups and letdowns. They help us to understand how we can get sidetracked in a setup or a letdown and don't move on to the humanizing phase. These stories are based on scriptural passages. They are meant to illumine the setups and letdowns that comprise all of our journeys, and they suggest how each may be a vital part of our never-ending search for God.

They are primarily stories of either setups or letdowns, depending on what appears to be emphasized in each story.

The Reflections

All of the reflections following the stories carry forward some of the ideas expressed here. However, reflections following the first set of stories specifically invite us to

Introduction: Setups and Letdowns

consider what promises but never quite delivers meaning. The second set of reflections challenges us to discover promise in the midst of disillusionment.

Setups

MINE

Luke 20:9: Jesus then began to tell the people the following parable: "A man planted a vineyard, leased it to tenant farmers, and went away for a long time."

"Magnificent!" sighed Ralph.
"Stunning!" whispered Reuben.
"Breathtaking! Simply breathtaking!" crowed Roger.
The three men stood in the center of the apple tree farm, which extended miles in every direction.
"What generosity! I, I, I'm speechless!" Ralph was speechless.
"Magnanimous! Mag-na-ni-mous! That's what he is: mag-na-ni- mous." Reuben enunciated like a teacher introducing a new word to his student.
"I'd say we're indebted to the man forever, not for a week, a month, a year, ten years, but forever!" Roger extended his arms, and raised them high on the word "forever." That served as a cue for the other two to lift their hands in praise and croon, "forever and forever" until they all crescendoed a minute later in nearly soprano voices.

And what was it that inspired such rapture? The owner of the apple farm, Mr. Good, had leased the land to them for a period of time, provided they tend the orchard and give him a certain percent of the profits from the yearly harvest of apples.

"Let's get on with tending Mr.—" Ralph had a lapse of memory as he tried to recall the owner's name.

"Ah! Ah! Ahhhh!" Roger shook his finger in mock shame. "It's Mr. Gander."

"Mr. Gaff, Roger, Mr. Gaff! How could you get the name wrong?" Reuben sniffed.

"Well anyway, *the owner*," all three conceded with just a touch of mockery in their voices.

Each went his own way to tend the parcel of property assigned to him by Mr. Good. That very day each posted signs with his name printed on them every ten feet around each's plot of land. They hadn't been on the property more than two weeks, however, than small picket fences separating the plots replaced the signs.

Standing on a tree ladder one afternoon, Ralph started to pick the apples off a branch extending over the property he tended but belonging to the tree on Reuben's side of the fence.

"What do you think you're doing?" The voice was Reuben's, and he was obviously upset. "That is *my* tree."

"Hmmmm," Ralph paused to think. "But the branch is on *my* side of the fence. And so the apples are *mine*," he concluded.

"They aren't," Reuben shot back.

"They are too," Ralph countered.

"Aren't!"

"Are!"

Mine

"Aren't!"

At this point Ralph grabbed a pruning saw resting on his ladder, quickly sawed off the offending branch and threw it onto Reuben's side. "You're right. It's yours," Ralph clapped his hands gleefully. "All yours, yours, yours!"

Hands on hips, Reuben stuck his tongue out at Ralph and muttered, "We'll see who owns what," and strode away in a huff.

It was only a matter of days before Reuben had built a fifteen- foot brick wall encircling the land he worked. Huge red letters painted on the side of the brick wall facing Ralph spelled MINE.

Meanwhile Ralph attempted to pick apples off branches extending from Roger's tree onto Ralph's side, just as he had done to Reuben's.

"Those apples are *mine, mine, mine,*" came a voice from a nearby treetop. It was Roger's. Periodically, he climbed up the top of a tree that he used as a lookout to spot possible intruders. Ralph's response to Roger was simply a repeat of what he had done earlier to Reuben. He lopped off the branch and threw it over the fence onto Roger's side.

Needless to say, Roger was furious, and within days he had erected a fifteen-foot wall with an electrically charged barbed wire fence mounted on the wall. Flags that read MINE, MINE, MINE flew atop numerous poles located on the fence. Not to be outdone by Reuben or Roger, Ralph built huge brick walls with barbed wire on top and towers two hundred feet in the air, which enabled Ralph to scan the horizon for miles to identify aliens.

Not satisfied with the walls encircling their plots of land, each man tied three or four huge wooden signs to the branches of each tree. Spelling MINE, the signs all but prevented the sun from shining on the trees. It was only a matter of weeks until the trees began to look terrible because the needed sunshine was blocked out by the high walls and signs. Their leaves dried up, and many of the apples remained green and stunted.

One afternoon as Ralph was carefully screening the countryside for the enemy, he spotted three men approaching the apple farm. By the manner of their dress they appeared to be servants of the owner of the orchard. The owner had heard from the neighboring farmers that the apple orchard was in bad repair. So he had decided to send his servants to advise Ralph, Roger, and Reuben how to restore the orchard to its original beauty. However, to Ralph the servants were the enemy and had no right to be there. He did nothing as he watched one burn himself trying to get through the electrically charged wire surrounding Roger's segment. Another accidentally tumbled off Reuben's brick wall. The third helped the other two, and all three sadly shook their heads before departing.

Unbeknownst to Ralph, Reuben and Roger had also been hiding in treetops and had seen the servants. All three of them were so alarmed at the prospect of strangers coming to the apple orchard that each regarded as his, they all began to watch day and night lest some stranger manage to come on the farm undetected. Frequently, each alone or together cried "Mine! Mine! Mine!" This went on for several days, until one afternoon they simultaneously spied a well-dressed young man riding in the direction of the farm on a beautiful black horse.

When the young man reached the entrance to the farm, he implored them for their sake and the good of

Mine

the orchard to lower their walls. All three began pelting him with stones. Immediately he fell to the ground and died. No sooner had this happened than all screeched in unison, "Mine! Mine! Mine!" So loud were they the echo reached the owner of the vineyard miles away. Sensing what had happened, the owner wept but decided to do nothing—for the time being. Why? Because he imagined the three men each by himself, each protecting what he thought was his, day in and day out, each fearful of the day when the owner finally would come to take way what was MINE. That, the owner thought, was truly what hell must be like.

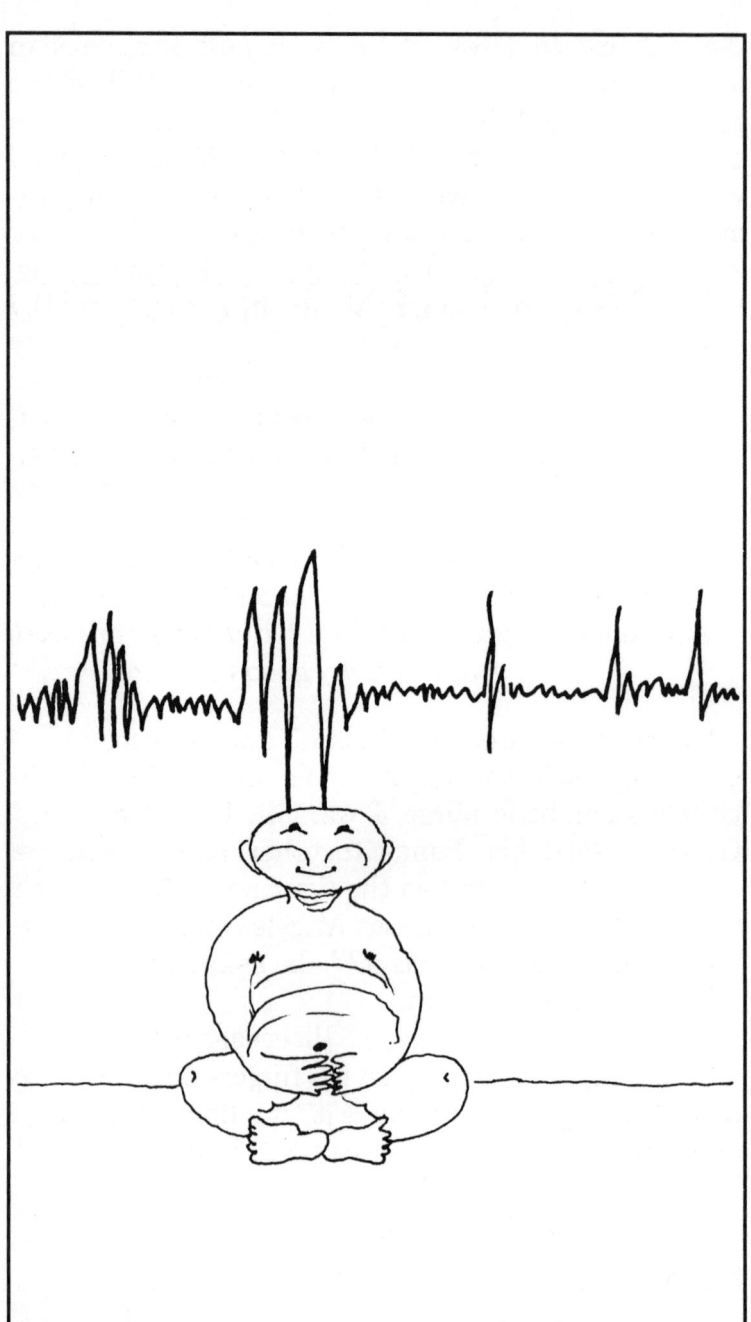

PORCELAIN PROBLEM

Luke 12:16-18: Jesus told them a parable in these words: "There was a rich man who had a good harvest. 'What shall I do?' he asked himself. 'I have no place to store my harvest. I know!' he said. 'I will pull down my grain bins and build larger ones. All my grain and my goods will go there.' "

"What an exquisite porcelain! The features are so detailed. I love the impish look on her face as she clutches her little purse. I want it. I must have it." Greta clasped her hands together as she and her husband, Max, examined the figurine in the porcelain shop on Front Street in Los Angeles one hot, smoggy afternoon. "How much is it?" she asked the clerk.

"Forty dollars, ma'am."

"Max, we've got to have it. Pleeeeaaase."

"Hmmm," Max drummed his fingers on the display case glass. "We've got to have it" is a line he had heard many times before when it came to buying figurines. "Well..."

"Please Max..." she pleaded.

"OK, OK," he relented, "but it's getting to the point where one of us is going to have to move out of the house! We don't have enough room for all these figurines."

"Max, don't be silly! We'll find room."

When Max and Greta arrived home that afternoon, Greta managed to find room, but just barely. There were crowds of Hummels, Lladros, and other foreign imports in every room of the house. Chinese goddesses competed for admiration alongside Christian madonnas; old men on crutches seemed to leer at young maidens on swings. Kings and queens, princes and princesses reigned over throngs of bizarre subjects wherever Greta could carve out a kingdom for them to reign. Huge identical Lladro hunting scenes, complete with huntsmen and women astride galloping horses preceded by hunting dogs, greeted guests at both the front and the rear entrances to the house.

Slowly, imperceptibly, but steadily, Greta's fascination with porcelains was changing her life. Sometimes she secretly managed to buy a figurine and sneak it inconspicuously among two or three others. At other times, the porcelain purchase was too obvious to hide. For example, when Max came home from work one afternoon, he asked Greta, "What happened to the matching chairs in the living room?"

"The chairs? Oh, I didn't think we needed them. We have enough already," Greta said casually.

"But all we've got left is the couch. You got rid of two chairs a month ago," Max protested. He had long since given up about always having to remove four or five refugee Hummels every time he wanted to sit on the couch to watch TV.

"Now don't worry, honey. If we need more chairs, we'll use the ones from the kitchen or borrow some from the neighbors."

Having dismissed Max's concern, she smiled and continued, "By the way, guess what I came across while I was shopping?" Max didn't answer. He didn't have to; he knew the answer already. "A llama Lladro! It's precious! See!" She pointed to the llama section of her bizarre menagerie installed on the living room window sill. Max could have sworn the new llama wore a triumphant look, as if claiming squatter's rights to its place on the sill. Greta continued, "It's not that easy to see now, but as soon as we get another figurine stand in the living room, we'll be able to display it better." Max didn't have to ask where it would go. He already guessed it would stand where the chairs had been.

In the weeks that followed, Max had to be out of town on business. During his absence, Greta invited a few of her friends over, never more than two at a time because there were so few chairs on which to sit. Moreover, the friends who did visit were given a guided tour of her porcelain collection; and the tour lasted the better part of the afternoon. No matter that she had given them the full tour on previous occasions; she felt compelled to update them on her recent acquisitions.

Invariably, she managed to direct all the conversations toward the subject of her figurines. If her friends talked about rice, she referred to the figurine of a Chinese maiden gracefully bending ankle deep in a rice field; if they wanted to talk about their children, she pointed to the angelic Hummel children kneeling, standing, bending, skipping, flirting, and hugging. Soon more and more of her friends declined her invitations.

The day Max returned, he was gripped with horror when he entered the house. Greta had gotten rid of the kitchen table and replaced it with a card table so she'd have more room for her kitchen gods. These were fat little Japanese buddhas holding their bellies as they grinned, laughed, and grimaced. But Max's horror turned to anger when he walked into the bedroom and saw not the bed but a Hummel crib set complete with Jesus, Mary, Joseph, the three kings, two sheep, two cows, and five shepherds.

Oblivious of his anger, Greta bubbled, "And Max, the rest of the family is coming tomorrow."

"What family?" Max looked at her dumbly.

"Jesus' extended family. The Hummels have just made Elizabeth, Zechariah, John the Baptist, and St. Ann," she announced proudly. "I'm so excited. It will be like a reunion."

"And where am I supposed to sleep during the reunion? In the basement?"

"That's not a bad idea, Max. I had thought about the back porch, but the basement is OK with me," she noted matter-of-factly.

"Oh yeh? Well it isn't OK with me! I've had it! Either you get rid of all this crap or I'm leaving. For good!"

"Hmmmm." Greta said nothing; she stood there silently.

"I don't believe this," Max hit his forehead over and over with the palm of his hand. "I simply don't believe this. You can't make up your mind, can you?"

Greta smiled. "Oh, but I have! It's taken me a long time to build up this collection. These are my children.

Porcelain Problem

They're precious, and I shouldn't give them up for anyone, not even you. These will last much longer than you. They'll be here forever."

Max shook his head. "You've made your choice. I'm leaving."

Within hours he had cleared out for good. The lack of furniture made the breakup significantly faster. Greta was delighted. Now she could bring in more figurines, expecially the white and red black-masked harlequins. By 11:30 that night they were smiling down on her from glass shelves in the new display case that had been Max's closet just a few hours earlier. Standing triumphantly in the crowded bedroom, she proclaimed, "We'll last forever. You'll see."

At 11:31 there were strong earth tremors in Los Angeles area. A news bulletin the next day indicated superficial damage in some sections on the city. Only in one instance was there a death: A woman with an unusually large number of porcelain figurines in her home was killed when some of the glass shelves and a number of harlequins came crashing down on her.

You are worth it!

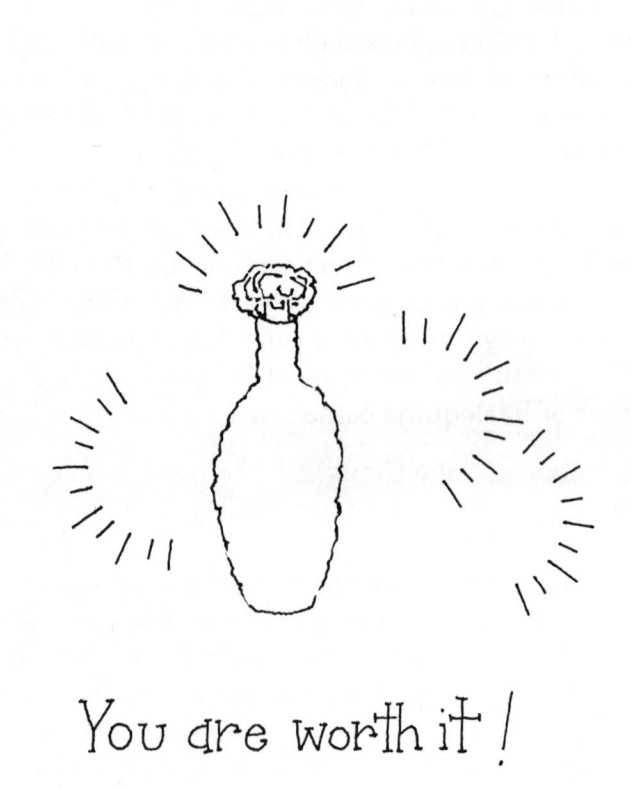

EXTRAVAGANCE

Matthew 26:6-8: While Jesus was in Bethany at the house of Simon the leper, a woman carrying a jar of costly perfume came up to him at table and began to pour it on his head. When the disciples saw this they grew indignant, protesting: "What is the point of such extravagance?"

"Bubble gum for all your friends! You spent your whole allowance to buy bubble gum for fifteen kids? Melissa, how could you?" Melissa's mom shook her head. "Maybe," she thought, "Melissa the adolescent will be less extravagant than Melissa the child."

"You what?"

"Ma, the guys like us more when we smell nice."

"But Melissa, you let all your friends spray themselves with my expensive *Parfum de Jerusalem*. Don't you think that's a little extravagant?" Melissa's mom wrung her hands. "Maybe," she prayed, "Melissa the young adult will be different from the adolescent. Maybe..."

"Melissa, you earn a lot of money managing a boutique, but you spend it all on gifts for friends." Melissa's mom was beginning to lose hope her daughter would ever change. "Why," she wondered, "is Melissa so extravagant?"

Certainly she and her husband weren't excessive in their lifestyle. They never behaved lavishly, not in spending money, giving compliments, or even showing affection. "Everything in moderation and only when deserved," was the advice Melissa's mother always gave her. Yet, Melissa didn't seem to get the message. She grew more, not less, extravagant.

"Five shirts for my birthday? One would have been plenty, Melissa." Her boyfriend was exasperated.

"You're worth it," she laughed. "Every penny of it!"

"Melissa, since we've started dating you've given me fifteen shirts, four pairs of cuff links and a belt with a gold-plated buckle—and that's just in two weeks! What are you trying to prove?"

"You're worth it," she laughed evasively.

But he didn't laugh and that ended the two-week relationship.

"Melissa, every time I come over here you've prepared enough food for ten people: three different soups, four entrees, and five kinds of dessert! That's more than I'm supposed to eat," objected her new portly boyfriend as he sat at the candelabra-decked dining table the sixth day into their relationship.

"You're worth it," Melissa smiled nervously.

"Melissa, you've had me over five nights in a row and each night it's the same story, more food and more food. My shirts and trousers don't fit anymore."

"I'll buy you a new set of clothes," she offered anxiously. "What size do you wear in suits, shirts, trousers, shoes, shorts, and belts?"

Extravagance

"Melissa," he begged, "you don't understand. What are you trying to prove?"

"That you're worth it," she smiled as she arranged and then rearranged the napkin on her lap.

"Not if I end up looking like a blimp," he thought, and that ended the six-day relationship.

Melissa's successive relationships fared no better. Her extravagance inspired awe, incredulity, and finally rejection from all of the men she dated. Over and over she'd tell them, "You're worth it," only to have them walk out of her life. However, more and more her laughter gave way to anxiety and her extravagances doubled.

A turn in this worsening state of affairs occurred one afternoon when she was introduced to a young rabbi named Jesus. She had already heard many good things about him and was particularly inspired by the generosity of spirit he was said to display toward everyone he met. She was determined his generosity would not go unrewarded. When finally they were introduced, Melissa blurted, "Sir, whatever your needs are, I would like to do whatever I can to help. Name the sizes, colors, and fabrics of the clothes you wear and I'll see to it you're supplied for a couple of years. And—"

"Wait, wait." Jesus raised a hand. "Do you think I want to open a clothing boutique?" he laughed.

"No, no. I..." Melissa stopped, gave a nervous laugh and with her eyes tearing up, cried "I don't know what is happening..." She tried to recover by continuing to press Jesus. "Sir, what can I give you or do for you? Please, please tell me what I can do."

Jesus listened sympathetically, and speaking softly, inquired, "What are you trying to prove?"

"What am I trying to prove?" She paused. "That you're worth it. Yes, that's it! That you're worth it!"

"That I'm worth it, or that you're worth it?"

Melissa's eyes opened wide, "That I'm worth it? I don't understand."

"Think about it. Think carefully, Melissa. And while you're thinking, I'm sure we can do something to help one another."

"What is that?" she asked warily.

"We can be friends, you and I, provided you give me nothing."

"Nothing?" Melissa whispered.

"Nothing," Jesus insisted.

"Never?"

Jesus grinned. "Well, not never! Let's say for two years. In the meantime just cool it with the gifts. Let's get to know one another just as we are, and not get smothered under all kinds of presents." He then pointed to the chairs. "Now let's sit and talk. Tell me about yourself."

And for the rest of the afternoon, Jesus and Melissa sat and enjoyed one another's company. When Melissa left Jesus, she felt a burden had been lifted from her shoulders. She hadn't had to plug herself with lavish gifts. She could just be herself. And this new experience sustained her whenever she was tempted to go overboard in getting anyone else to accept her.

Two years later Melissa decided it was time to give Jesus a special gift, the little extravagance he promised she could give him some day. Her desire was prompted as much by her newfound freedom to be herself as it was by her fear that Jesus might not be around much

Extravagance

longer. It didn't take a genius to see how his enemies were pressing in on every side, and she sensed how quiet and sad he had become in recent weeks.

So one afternoon she chose to revert to her former extravagant way. She bought Jesus a huge decanter of very expensive perfume and personally delivered it to a party she knew Jesus was attending. Melissa wanted him to use this perfume for himself, but knowing his generous nature she feared he would give it away. Consequently, she snuck up behind him at table and without a word poured the perfume directly onto his head. Startled, Jesus looked up, then took her hand in his and kissed it. Looking around the room, he noticed his own friends were upset.

"What is the point of such extravagance?" they muttered. "This could have been sold for a good price and the money given to the poor."

Pained by their criticism, Jesus said, "Why do you criticize the woman? It is a good deed she has done for me. The poor you will always have with you, but you will not always have me. By pouring this perfume on my body, she has helped me prepare for my death." Then, looking into Melissa's eyes, Jesus struck an extravagant note, "I assure you, whenever the good news is proclaimed throughout the world, what you did will be remembered."

That afternoon two generous spirits had competed and outdone one another in love.

Reflection

I'm really somebody because of what I own.

It is an illusion that we are what we own. Illusion takes the form of possession in "Porcelain Problem" and "Mine," while it masks itself as giving in "Extravagance." In all three stories, the compulsive taking and giving suggests addictive behavior.

We can speculate that Roger, Ralph, and Reuben in "Mine," and Greta in "Porcelain Problem" wanted to acquire and hoard because it was their only way of establishing their importance. Possessions prop up weak selves with an illusion of expanding selves. Our possessions give us tangible proof that we are important and that our importance expands with the more we acquire. Yet, what is ironic in "Mine" and "Porcelain Problem" is how the characters are actually increasingly constricted by the clutter. Consequently, while the illusion of the expanding self prevails, the reality is that the selves are contracting and being overwhelmed by "things."

Interestingly enough, this illusion of expansion, coupled with the reality of constriction, might be a concrete way of illustrating how addicted persons continue pursuing the object of addiction despite the suffering it brings. They want more because it promises more; but they enjoy it less because it delivers less; and in the exchange they are rendered more and more impotent. Feeling increasingly depleted and guilty, they become ever more dependent on their addiction to provide the illusion of a strong, solid self.

Unfortunately, the characters in "Mine" and "Porcelain Problem" never experienced the disillusionment that would have provided insight into their destructive behavior. Nor did they ever achieve an understanding of their addiction as having its origin in a fundamentally religious drive to find fulfillment within a larger reality. Reflecting on their boundless need to incorporate (that is, acquire) might have led to the insight that what they really desired was to be incorporated or taken in by a larger reality. Blind to what was happening, they invested in their addiction an energy that could only have been absorbed by that much larger reality. As a result, their addictions, like all addictions, became so highly charged that disaster was inevitable.

In "Extravagance" the situation isn't so dangerous because Melissa's compulsion to give was checked by Jesus. As she reflected on her motives, she began to realize how her extravagance was actually a need to be accepted by others. Given this insight, she was later able to give freely out of a sense of adequacy, not depletion and need. But she first had to be disillusioned. Jesus insisted she relate to him as one presence to another rather than as someone to be pleased and appeased through gifts. He would not permit himself to be placed on a pedestal and idolized.

What kind of a statement are we making about ourselves through the clothes, books, furniture, cars, jewelry, cosmetics, etc., we buy? Do we feel more important because of the learned books in our library, or more powerful because of the cars we drive? Do the high pricetags on the shirts, dresses, coats, and shoes we purchase tell us we are high priced?

Do we experience a compulsion to get or to give; what does this tell us about our sense of self worth? Does it mask the living illusion that we are somebody because of what we own?

POWER PLAY

Mark 10:35-37: Zebedee's sons, James and John, approached Jesus. "Teacher," they said, "we want you to grant our request." "What is it?" he asked. They replied, "See to it that we sit, one at your right and the other at your left, when you come into your glory."

"Can you imagine? The nerve!"

"Who do they think they are anyway? Hotshots?"

"Not even bothering to consults us! As if we didn't matter!"

They were all hopping mad that afternoon at Abe's Corner Bar. Phil had overheard the Zebedee brothers hassling Jesus for choice seats in the kingdom when the glory days would arrive. John had done the talking.

" 'Put Jim on your right and me on your left. You won't be sorry. We'd help you run the show more efficiently.' " He sounded convincing, and to bolster his chances he added, 'Getting those glory seats would be an added incentive for us to do a first-rate job here and now!' "

Jesus hadn't granted their requests, but that didn't prevent the uproar that followed. Phil's face was red as a beet when he told the other disciples what had happened. After they had taken turns venting their feelings, Jude proposed they all approach Jesus and settle once and for all where each would stand once the kingdom commenced.

"Stand?" Nathaniel asked.

"Yes, for example, what's going to be your title? Or Bart's? Naturally, I'd expect to be associate director."

"Associate director?" Nat sounded suspicious. "Who's the director?"

"Jesus of course," Jude replied.

"Then I'd like to be assistant director," Bart blurted.

"Assistant director?" Jude and Nat puzzled simultaneously.

"Yes."

"What's the assistant's relation to the director?" Jude eyed Bart suspiciously.

"He assists the director," Bart answered matter-of-factly.

"I know that," Jude answered sharply. "I mean is the assistant director more important that the associate director?"

"Well of course," Bart answered. "Do you think I'd settle for the position of associate director?"

"And what makes you think I'd settle for having the assistant director taking precedence over the associate?" Jude asked heatedly.

"Fellas, I think we can understand now why we need the good services of an executive coordinator for the kingdom, someone who stands head and shoulders above the associate and the assistant directors," Phil was now ready to make his pitch.

"Why do we need an executive coordinator? And what's this talk about standing above the associate director?" Jude's voice had an increasingly aggressive edge to it.

"A coordinator, Jude, is responsible for harmonizing everybody toward a common action. And an executive coordinator harmonizes in an executive way," Phil explained without really saying anything. Admiring himself in a mirror over the bar, he continued, "Of course, some of us have the talent for being executive coordinators, and some of you don't."

"And of all the talented persons suited for the position, *you* are by far the best and brightest candidate for executive coordinator. Right?" Nat's sarcasm was obvious to everyone in the room except Phil.

"You said it!" Phil winked. "Yes, I'm the best candidate for the position. They're going to love me. They—"

"How can you stand there and be so assured you're going to be executive coordinator?" Jude demanded.

"Yeh, don't you have any modesty whatsoever? Don't—"

"Gentlemen, gentlemen." Nat didn't have time to finish his question because Andrew was ready to make his own proposal. "Don't worr-ee!! Don't arr-gue! When I'm appointed Vice Regent, I'll straighten out the whole matter!"

"Vice Regent?" Brows furrowed, Jude, Bart, and Nat hustled to balance this new position with their own.

"What is a Vice Regent?" Nat asked cautiously.

"A stand-in."

"For what?"

"In this case, for Jesus."

"A stand-in!" Bart blurted a second time. "A stand-in for Jesus? Are you kidding? You mean when Jesus is busy elsewhere, you'll be the big matzo?"

"Yup." He straightened his tunic while Jude's eyes widened.

"And get served beef bourguignon first?"

"Yup." And rapping his fingers on the counter, he added nonchalantly, "As well as calling on a whole squadron of wings to do my bidding." Matt gulped.

"Even," Peter paused and lowered his head reverently as he posed the number-one question on everybody's mind, "even talking directly to," he pointed upward, then whispered, "the Big One?"

"Yehhh!" Andrew sighed.

"No! No! No!" From all over the room the disciples yelled their objections to Andrew's claim to becoming Vice Regent. Crushing their beer cans with a facility none had shown at earlier gatherings, each boasted of how deserving he was and the qualities only he could bring to the position.

"I've got the brains."

"Yeh, but I've got the looks."

"So what? I'm more charming."

"Who cares about charm? I've got good business sense."

"Stop this nonsense!" a voice rang out. It was Jesus' voice. He had entered unnoticed and was listening to their bickering. "Who do you think you're working for? The First Jerusalem Bank? What do you think I'm looking for? Preening prelates or primping princes? There are already enough of them dancing heavily on the backs of others. What I need are people who'll gladly shoulder one another's burdens. Develop that skill to the hilt and then you'll be number one with me. So let's hear no more talk of who's who in the kingdom. We've more important things to do." Jesus smiled, and when he smiled the tension eased. "Well now," Jesus paused, searched the disciples' faces and laughed. "any assistant, associate, or executive directors here who'd like to serve us a round of beer? Who knows? If you do it royally, you just may be sitting at my right hand after all!"

Reflection

I'm really somebody because of my position.

The illusion that we are the role we play is not an illusion we readily surrender. We achieve status through our work, academic achievements, and other social accomplishments. Often it takes years and a great deal of effort to win recognition for what we have done. No wonder that we tend to identify our status and role in society with *who* we are. Person and role merge so completely that we easily forget we are not what we do nor are we the titles before our names.

In "Power Play" the disciples attempt to establish their importance in the future kingdom by assigning themselves prominent roles. Consequently, the kingdom becomes the arena for the kind of power plays so prominent on earth. Yet, as Jesus reminds them, the kingdom is not an extension of the usual ploys people use in becoming important. Rather, importance in the kingdom is based on service to others, not mastery through the assumption of titles and the heavy-handed imposition of authority.

Do we pull rank? Do we let others know who's boss? Do we make it clear where we stand in the pecking order? And do we keep people in their place by reminding them who they are and who we are and how we got to be where we are? What happens inside when others don't seem to know to whom they are speaking? Are we angry? Upset? Do we still live with the illusion we are somebody because of our position?

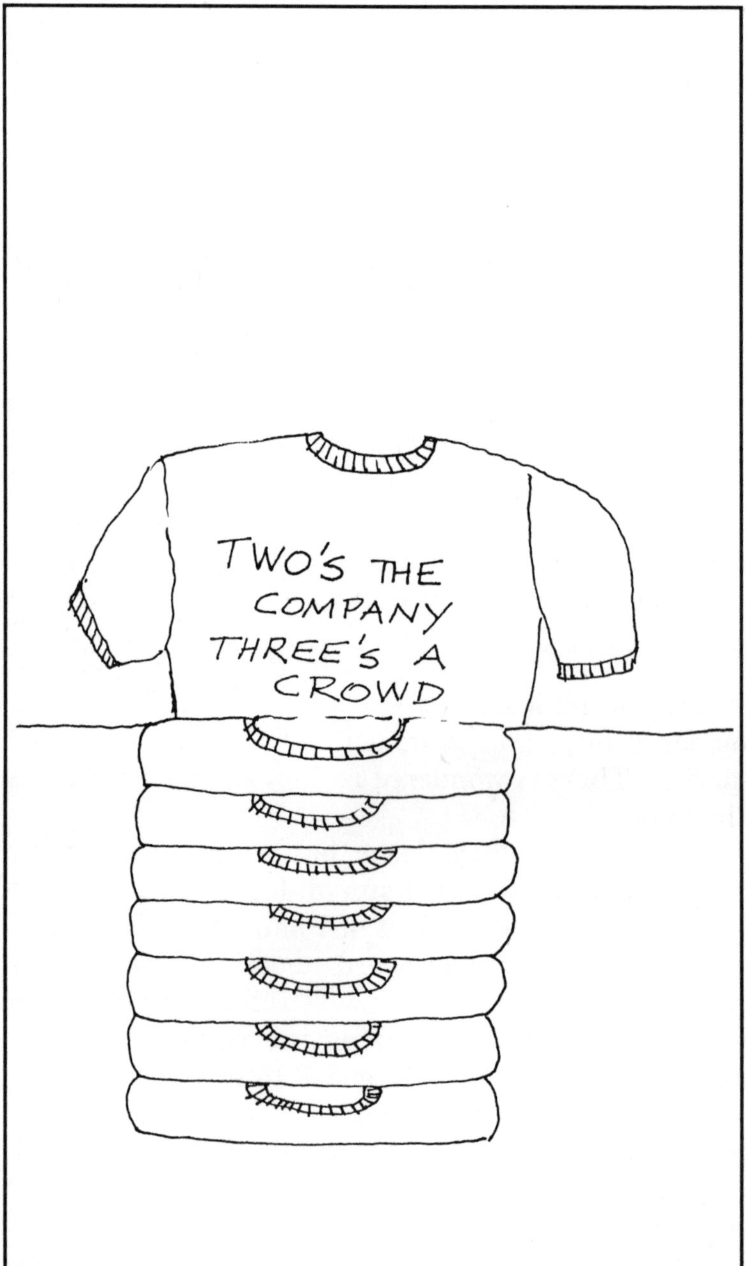
TWO'S THE
COMPANY
THREE'S A
CROWD

THE COMPANY

Mark 9:38-40: John said to Jesus, "Teacher, we saw a man using your name to expel demons and we tried to stop him because he is not of our company." Jesus said in reply, "Do not try to stop him. No man who performs a miracle using my name can at once speak ill of me."

"Do you think Jesus would mind if we had the backs of our tunics monogrammed *I Follow Jesus* in sequins?" Thomas wondered as they sat on a bench in the park.

"Sequins are a little flashy, but I think he'd like the idea," Jude answered. Four of Jesus' disciples had gathered in the south end of Pilate Park that afternoon because they had heard rumors of unidentified people casting out demons. To their horror, the strangers did so by invoking the name of "their" Jesus, and the disciples intended to stop them.

"Rhinestones might be better," Bart advised. "It's more macho. By the way, I think Phil's idea of having rings inscribed with *Jesus Is My Personal Lord And Savior* would really set us off from those who don't belong."

"Great idea, Bart!" Tom was elated. "And whenever we meet, we could use a rallying cry that would let others know who we are and where we stand."

"What did you have in mind, Tom?" Bart asked.

"Something like 'Praise the Lord! Rah! Rah! Rah! Sis Coom Bah!'"

"Hmmmm. Sounds interesting. Praise the Lord! Rah! Rah! Rah! Sis Coom Bah!" Bart was impressed.

They all sounded in unison. "Praise the Lord! Rah! Rah! Rah! Sis Coom Bah!"

"I think we've got some good ideas here, fellas," Jude spoke approvingly. Monogrammed *I Follow Jesus* tunics; *Jesus Is My Personal Lord And Savior* rings; a 'Praise The Lord!' rallying cry. I—"

"Wait," Tom interrupted. "Look over there! Is that who I think it is?" The disciples turned their attention to a little white-haired lady addressing a small crowd about one-hundred feet from where the disciples were sitting. Dressed in a clean, white robe and standing on a wooden crate, she had placed her hands on the head of a man considerably taller than herself.

"That's one of them, all right," Jude waved his hand excitedly. "Let's go!"

The four disciples hurried over to the gathering and stood off toward the side as the woman continued praying over the man in front of her. "Out, I say. Go out of him in Jesus' name—"

That was the signal they had been waiting for. "Stop! Stop!" Jude yelled. "You can't do that!"

Startled, all in the crowd turned and stared at Jude.

"I can't do what?" the woman puzzled.

"You can't use Jesus' name to get rid of someone's demons!"

"Why can't I?"

The Company

The four disciples lost no time hurling reasons why she couldn't.

"You have no credentials!"

"Nor the right formula!"

"And you're placing your hands improperly!"

"Have you really accepted Jesus into your heart?"

"Or in your mind?"

"What's important is you can't grant a bona fide expulsion because you don't belong to the club! You're not one of the boys!" Jude concluded triumphantly.

"Yeh! Yeh! She's not of our company," the four applauded Jude.

"No, I don't belong to your club. And I'm certainly not one of the boys. But from what I know about Jesus, he doesn't care about club membership and rules the way you do. I'm sure he wouldn't mind my using his good name to help a needy person."

"Right on! Right on!" It was the small crowd's turn to applaud, and as they did the little woman resumed her work.

"In Jesus' name, I command you to leave this man!" It was only a matter of seconds before the possessed man smiled and thanked the woman for what she had done. The disciples were incensed as they stormed off to the little house where Jesus was staying for a day.

"Boy! Wait til Jesus hears about this," Tom warned.

"Yeh! What right did she have to be good to someone without getting permission from the proper authority?" Bart objected.

"The demon will probably catch on and come back for a longer stay once it discovers that she didn't go through the right channels," Tom assured them as he

55

SETUPS

flung open the front door of the house. The four marched into the living room and startled Jesus, who was resting on the sofa.

"Jesus, we know you're going to be really upset, but we have some bad news," Bart said gravely.

"What's wrong?" Jesus asked as he sat up and readied himself for the worst.

"Who's going to tell him?" Bart looked at the others.

"Tell me what?" Jesus asked impatiently.

Shaking his head at the others' lack of courage, Bart cleared his throat. "Jesus, we saw a woman using your name to expel a demon! Of course we tried to stop her because she doesn't belong to the company, but—"

"The company?" Jesus scratched his head. He had no idea what company Bart was talking about.

"I mean she's not one of us, you know," Bart explained.

"Oh, oh," Jesus nodded. "Our company. Hmmmmm. Well, that's OK!" Jesus waved a hand and stretched out once more on the sofa.

"What?" the others exclaimed in unison.

"I said, 'That's OK!' Why stop anyone who wants to do good in my name? That's great! The more the merrier. Look, anyone who isn't against us belongs to our, er, 'company' as you put it. I don't care whether that person hangs around with us or not. What's in the heart is what counts with me."

The disciples stood there silently; they looked sheepishly at Jesus and one another.

"Jesus," Tom said softly, "I think we owe someone an apology. Right fellas?"

"Right," they answered feebly.

"Who are *we* talking about?" Jesus had an impish look on his face.

"Just someone. Bye, Jesus. We'll be back." And the four disciples slipped out and returned to the park. They wanted a certain person to know they had made room for more company.

Reflection

I'm really somebody because of the company I keep.

The above illusion is as pervasive as the air we breathe. Churches, political parties, unions, country clubs, fraternities, sororities, etc., are all facets of the company we keep. But the potentially disastrous illusion here is elitism. When we demean others (outsiders) and read in their differences (our superiority), then we are elitist.

In "The Company," the disciples' identified themselves with externals rather than with doing good. The accouterments of monogrammed T-shirts, rings, and slogans became their means of self-definition. And if anyone else claimed their prerogatives without regard for the externals, as did the lady in her exorcism, he or she was considered intimidating. The disciples' differences were more quirks rather than clear signs of superiority.

Identity based on externals is a shaky identity at best and signals an underlying insecurity. This insecurity is implied in the remarks of people extolling the virtues of one religious tradition over another. "We have what you don't" is the game of one-upmanship or "top dog/bottom dog," which betrays an uneasy, timorous self behind a facade of religious bravado.

Our ability to stand back and offer constructive criticism to whatever group we belong is a healthy sign of self-worth. And this is a far cry from living the illusion that we are important because of the company we keep.

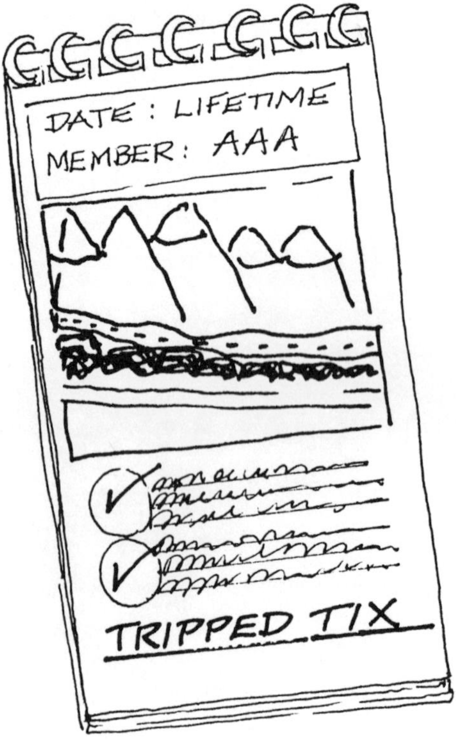
DATE : LIFETIME
MEMBER : AAA
TRIPPED TIX

TRIPPED UP

Matthew 22:35-36: ...and one of them, a lawyer, in an attempt to trip him up, asked Jesus, "Teacher, which commandment of the law is the greatest?"

Sol was his name. Solomon, really, named after the great Solomon who knew how to carry out the law in all wisdom. As a youngster, Sol had heard the great prayer, "Shema, Israel, Hear, O Israel, You shall love the Lord your God with all your heart, with all your mind, and with all your soul." Day after day, Sol's parents recited the prayer. So, too, day after day, with a song in his heart, Sol wondered how he might love this God with all his heart, and all his mind, and all his soul. With a light heart, he dreamed dreams about what he might do and be. Finally, it came to him: He'd be a lawyer. As a lawyer, he could faithfully interpret God's law. Then he and others could love God with more and more of their hearts and minds and souls. And so it was that Sol became a lawyer.

Everyone said that if anyone could win hearts and minds and souls to love God above all else, it was Sol. So smart was Sol in the law of God, he knew the law backward and forward, every jot and tittle. He could quote chapter and verse for you, so smart was he in the law. And he was well versed in what the great rabbis had said about the law. Sol pored over his law books; night after night he read the commentaries.

All this was very admirable. Unfortunately, it didn't leave him much time for his wife and children. Often his wife would come to his room and tell him that she and the children missed him and wanted him to come out and enjoy the sun and the beach with them. Well, Sol would look up from his books, gently lay his finger aside his nose, and patiently hear his wife out. Then with his gift for picking out flaws in arguments, he would show her precisely where she was wrong.

"So, it is good to enjoy the sun?" he'd ask.

"Why yes," replied his wife, brightening at the thought that perhaps he would join them.

"Then how much better to enjoy the Maker of the sun, by studying his Law." He had tripped her up! Shaking her head, his wife would leave the room, wishing that he'd show them just a fraction of the love he had in his heart and soul and mind for God.

And the other lawyers? They really admired Sol because he was so sharp, so eloquent, and because he could argue so well. But on the other hand, they were suspicious of him. He never cared to chat with them or to just sit and relax with them. No, his only interest was exposing their faulty reasoning in discussions, formal and informal alike. And then tripping them up. So what if at times he appeared to be overzealous in defending God's law—wasn't this a sign of wholehearted love for God? So what if Sol became gradually more serious and sober in his defense of God's law—after all, keeping the law of God was a serious matter, and loving God was no laughing matter.

Tripped Up

He became a regular watchdog of the law. Somebody had to watch the less zealous lest they try to get away with anything. More and more, he made it a point to tell people how to observe the Sabbath and how not to observe it; what to eat and what not to eat; what to wear and what not to wear; the kinds of taxes they were to pay and the kinds not to pay. And if they complained, he would listen with his finger resting gently on the side of his nose. Then, when they were finished he would show them where they were wrong, how they had gone astray. "If you find it a burden to carry out the law of God, then you are refusing to carry God Himself in your heart. For are not God and the Law one and the same?" And so he caught them off guard. Tripped them up! Why? Because he loved God above everything else, in heart and mind and soul.

Of course, at times he felt the strain of it all. Once they brought a woman caught in adultery. So many excuses, so many explanations! Yes, arguments were put forward in her defense. Mercy would have been an easy way out. "Ah, my heart goes out to you," he said to her. No sooner did he say this than he became painfully aware he had been caught off guard by his unchecked sentiment for the woman. How could he have felt this way, for anyone less than God? He had almost tripped up himself! Then and there he resolved no arguments must sway him; he showed the others where they were wrong and he pointed out their weaknesses. Finally, he rendered judgment on the woman because he loved God so much!

Sol's reputation spread as the one who knew how to decide which laws were more important than others, which laws appeared to contradict one another, and which interpretation to give some obscure law no one

SETUPS

had ever heard of. No one had mastered the intricacies and complexities of the law better than Sol. Certainly no one could compete in pointing out the difference between serving God's interests and catering to the whims of his creatures.

So it was only a matter of time before Sol was tapped on the shoulders by people who, like himself, were concerned about God's love. They were the protectors and guardians of the Law. Now Sol became one of them, one of the elite, the separate ones, the Pharisees. Along with them he helped to keep the less-informed informed about the law. He kept them in line and showed them the way. Sol wished they had the love of God in heart and soul and mind as he did. Thank God, he thought, that he and a few others loved God so fervently, so zealously, so religiously. But then, who else knew the law, interpreted it, and saw to its enforcement as well as Sol and the group he joined? And because he knew it so well, it was only right that the others came to him one day with a request. They wanted him to show his ability to trip up yet another person—Jesus of Nazareth.

Jesus of Nazareth? He had heard of this popular rabbi, popular no doubt because he had catered to the needs of the people, caved in to their every desire. Jesus spoke intimately of loving God in one breath but in the next he treated God's Law as if it were unimportant. He healed people on the Sabbath when no healing was allowed. He spoke about lilies of the field, about mustard trees, about parties and banquets instead of upholding God's law. Sol stiffened as he thought about Jesus. Yes, he was going to teach this Jesus a lesson. He was going to trip him up and show him where he was wrong.

Tripped Up

So the next day Sol went to the temple precincts where Jesus was preaching to a large crowd. Sol was late as he approached the crowd, but he heard Jesus speaking about caring for the neighbor, nothing about loving God, which was the most important law in Sol's life. Sol let Jesus speak for a while. Then from the back of the crowd, Sol wet his lips, cleared his throat, and interrupted Jesus. In an attempt to trip him, he asked Jesus which was the greatest commandment. Jesus looked at him, knowing that this one wanted to catch him off guard. Jesus told him, "You shall love the Lord your God with all your heart, with all your mind..." and then with particular care, Jesus added, "and your neighbor as yourself."

Sol stepped back. Jesus had answered by joining the two commandments. What Jesus was saying sounded preposterous: Loving God and loving the neighbor were not to be separated. If you loved God, you loved your neighbor. "If you love your neighbor, you love God?" he laughed to himself, and then he stopped. Sol got the point, good lawyer that he was.

The reverse of that would also be true: If you tripped up the neighbor, tried to expose him, in effect you were trying to trip up...God. Trip up God? Catch God? Do God in? In a flash scenes from the past came back to him. Scenes of the young woman caught in adultery, scenes with his wife, so many scenes where he had tried to catch people off guard, all because he said he loved God. But if what Jesus said were true, then what he had done to them, he was in fact doing to God! A heavy feeling came over him as he sunk down on the ground.

The question that began to burn in Sol's mind and heart and soul was this: Since he had not loved his neighbor as he thought he loved his God, had he ever really loved God after all? Good lawyer that he was, he knew the answer even as he thought of the question, and he began to feel pain in his ankles. For he realized that the only person he had tripped up all these years was himself.

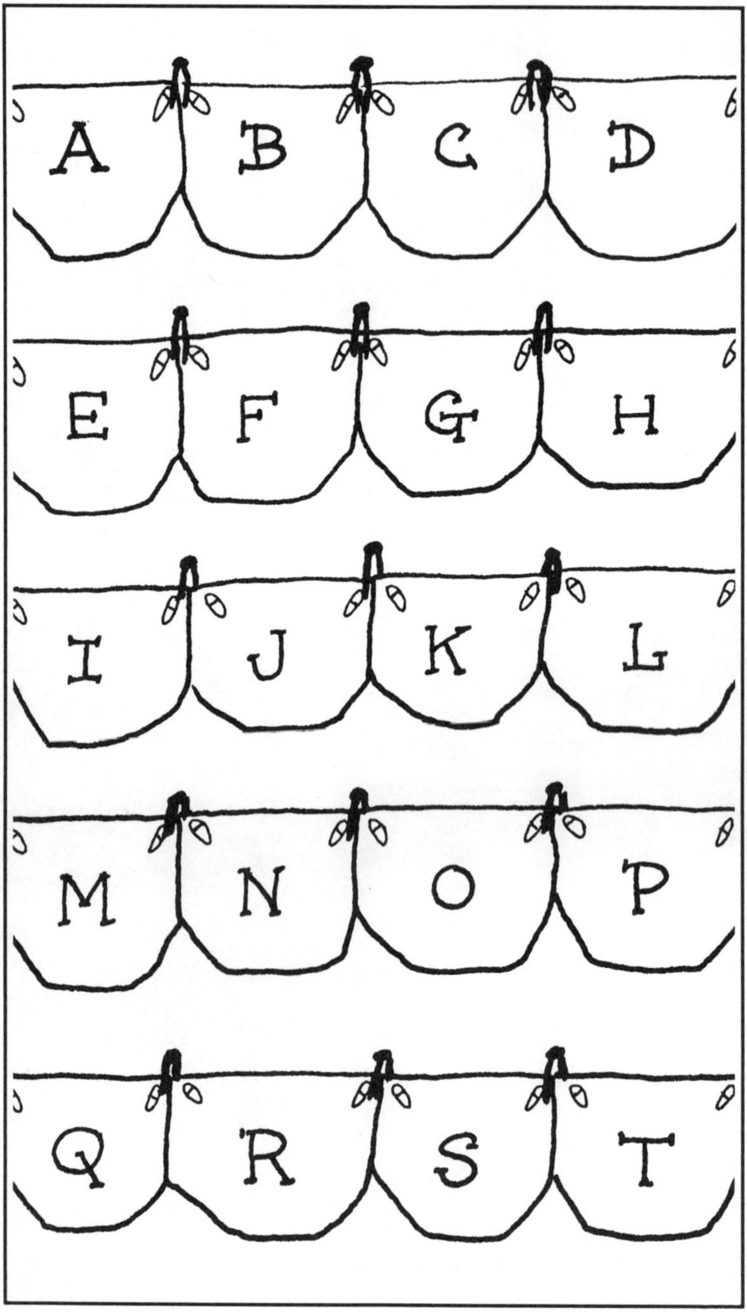
A B C D
E F G H
I J K L
M N O P
Q R S T

THE KINGDOM

Mark 10:13-15: People were bringing their little children to him to have him touch them, but the disciples were scolding them for this. Jesus became indignant when he noticed it and said to them: "Let the children come to me and do not hinder them. It is to just such as these that the kingdom of God belongs."

"We've got to get organized. More disciplined! This is serious business. We haven't got time for fooling around, for fiddle- faddle." Peter paced the floor, going over strategy for a rally Jesus was leading the next day outside Jericho.

"Peter, you have pinpointed the problem," Nathaniel heartily agreed. "For a long time now, I've said to myself we're getting a *little* too loose, a *little* too free and easy. I bet none of us knows exactly what our daily schedule is for this week. Does anybody know? Does *anybody*?" Nathaniel had thrown a curve ball; all of the disciples tried and failed to recall what lay ahead for that week. "See," Nathaniel swept the room with his hand, "No one knows. No one."

"Good point, Nat," Peter agreed. "We are a *little* too loose in the area of accountability. Which one of us is able to explain his whereabouts for the last three days: time spent eating, sleeping, reading, preaching, going to the bathroom; money spent on necessities, frivolities? Have we frittered away our time?" Once more the disciples raced through mental gymnastics, attempting to recall how they had spent the last couple of days.

"What can we do to be more effective, more cost and time efficient?" Andrew wondered.

Never at a loss for words, Nathaniel raised his hand. "I'd like to suggest we begin by carrying *little* pads of paper and note what we do and where we do it every fifteen minutes. As a reminder, each of us will wear a buzzer that goes off automatically every fifteen minutes. I'd like to further suggest each of us pair up with a buddy to whom we report and who evaluates us on how well we've spent our time. Checks and double checks! That's what we need."

"I really think we're getting somewhere. We should have had a serious discussion a long time ago. But now comes a real sensitive issue." Peter's face grew serious. The other disciples straightened up in their chairs, folded their arms, and waited. "Fellas, we've all got to be more serious when Jesus is preaching. I've seen some of you laughing during his sermons. I'm not going to name names, but golly, don't you think we owe it to Jesus to give him our undivided attention? Now I know he likes to tell jokes, but let's show a little restraint in our laughter. Do you think the kingdom is for clowns? Do you want to go down in the books as goof-offs? I certainly wouldn't want my history to read I was someone always putting my foot in my mouth. I—"

The Kingdom

Peter was interrupted by uncontrollable giggling from somewhere in the room. Spying the culprit, Peter demanded, "What's so funny, Matthew? What are you laughing at?"

"I'm not laughing, Peter. It's my tunic. It tickles," Matthew blurted as he tried biting his sleeve to hold back more giggling. He knew that if he had anything to do with writing Peter's history, people would have a laugh or two. Peter sensed the real reason for the giggling but didn't press it. He didn't need the added indignity of having his previous misjudgments broadcast to the group. "As I was saying..." Peter tried to refocus but had forgotten what he had been saying.

"You were talking about giggling a *little* too much during Jesus' sermons," Nathaniel reminded him.

"Oh yes, well, I think I've covered that matter. I—" Once more, Nathaniel had his hand in the air. "What is it, Nat?" Peter sounded a little impatient, probably because next to himself Nathaniel was doing all the talking.

"One other *little* matter we ought to discuss are the logistics for handling the crowds."

"Yes, yes, Nat. That is a problem. Crowd control is very—"

"I say keep them orderly by having them sit in rows A through Z. Immediately after Jesus is finished preaching, give everybody paper and pencil to write down any questions and then submit the questions to a screening committee of two who in turn will pass on the important ones to Jesus. And after the service is over, instead of the crowd rushing Jesus, we can line up everyone who'd like to shake his hand." Nathaniel was a goldmine of suggestions.

"OK, OK," Peter's voice betrayed pique. He thought *he* was supposed to be running the meeting, not Nathaniel. "I have one last item before adjourning, fellas. A lot of kids come up and bother Jesus before, during, and after his preaching. I know he doesn't object, but it must bother him. It sure bothers me, all those kids making faces and squirming around. Let's be gentle, but let's insist that the kids play with their Tinkertoys back near the horses and donkeys and not be nuisances—"

Peter stopped. He thought he heard light snoring. Sure enough, two or three of the disciples had dozed off, and others were nodding their heads. "Are you with me, fellas?" Peter challenged as he glared from one to the next.

"Eh? What was that? Yeh, we heard you," they muttered. They had heard more than they cared to hear and wanted to call it a day. Sensing further discussion would be useless, Peter decided it was time to adjourn.

"OK fellas, I'll see you bright and early for the rally. Tomorrow we'll put into effect everything we've discussed here."

The next day the disciples ran into opposition from the person they least expected: Jesus. He thought Nathaniel's ideas for crowd control were ridiculous, but not wanting to hurt his feelings, stated his objection tactfully. "I like people to mingle and get to know one another, Nat. Asking them to organize themselves into rows from A to Z or lining them up to shake my hand is too formal for me." But what Jesus objected to most strongly was the attempt to keep the kids segregated with the horses. This signaled a serious misunderstanding of what God's reign was about.

The Kingdom

"What do you think you're doing keeping the kids away from me? I want them around me. They love to play and so do I. What's gotten into you? You've all gotten serious—too serious. Especially you, Peter and Nat." Matthew put his hand to his mouth when Jesus mentioned Peter's name. He had to bite his lip to prevent himself from erupting into laughter as he scrambled for a pad and pencil to jot down a couple of notes. Jesus continued as Peter stared daggers in Matthew's direction. "We could learn a lesson or two from these kids. The kingdom isn't a place of business but the dance of children in the sun. There's enough gloom and doom here without adding more in the name of the kingdom. Loosen up or you'll miss out on it because the ticket for getting in is knowing how to play." Looking in the direction of Nathaniel and Peter, Jesus smiled and urged, "C'mon, c'mon, smile! It won't hurt you."

Nathaniel and Peter smiled sheepishly. "So much for yesterday's meeting," Peter muttered. Then looking around he said, "OK fellas. It's time to play with the kids."

The Kingdom Day had begun.

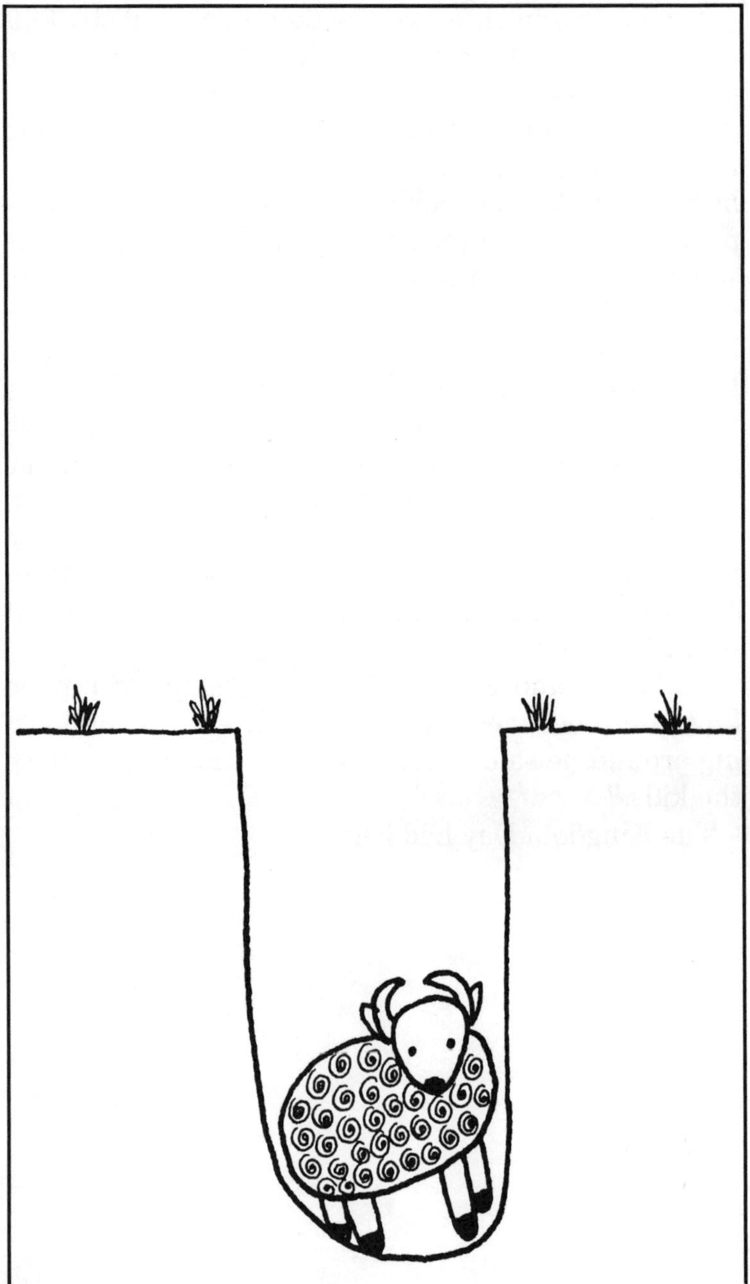

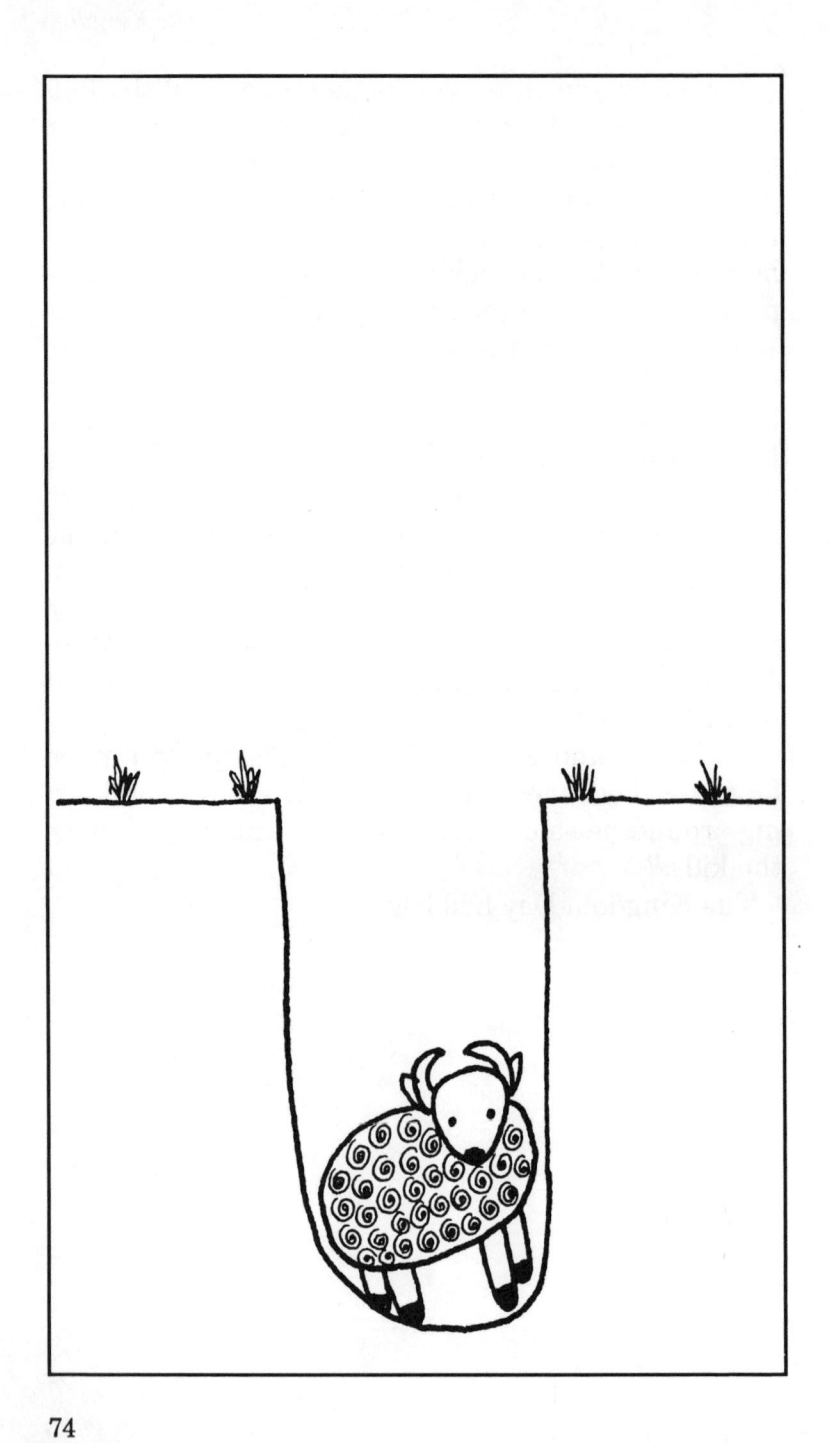

FAR RIGHT

Matthew 12:9-10: Jesus left that place and went into their synagogue. A man with a shriveled hand happened to be there, and they put this question to Jesus, hoping to bring an accusation against him: "Is it lawful to work a cure on the sabbath?"

Far right! All Lem's friends knew that's where he stood on any issue they discussed. As far right as anyone could go.

Once a friend asked him, "Lem, what's your understanding of the law regarding—"

"We need the strictest laws we can enforce, and the most rigid order we can maintain," Lem lectured even before he heard what issue his friend had in mind. Whatever the topic or the issue was didn't really matter. Tithing, toilet training, dietary laws, moral education, dress codes—all equally needed to be rigidly ordered by the strictest legislation.

Moreover, there could never be room for compromise. " 'Right,' I say. 'Go right, young man, go right,' " he ordered when his son was debating which way to move on an issue. "Don't be wishy-washy. We don't want any left-leaning liberals in our family. Not on your life!" And whenever he argued with his friends regarding healing on the Sabbath, Lem invariably took the strictest, most conservative approach. "No healing on the Sabbath," he told them. "Absolutely none! Permit it just once, then we're going to see everybody making up excuses to heal on the Sabbath. Then where will we be? With all kinds of healed people walking the streets?"

Lem's logic left his friends shaking their heads in disbelief. "He's afraid of too many healed people walking the streets! Can you believe that?" they moaned.

Lem's wife, Fannie, had the heaviest burden of all. She had to listen to his harangues against the limp-wristed, left-wing liberals and his defense of the God-fearing, patriotic right-wing rednecks. On Monday, Wednesday, and Friday, it was The-Value-Of-Carrying-An-Assortment-Of-Knives-For-Self-Protection monologue and on Tuesday, Thursday, and Saturday, The-Glory-Of-Being-Told-What-To-Do-And-Liking-It pitch. Why, it got so bad at the meal table that Fannie and the kids had to avoid mentioning any point of view that veered ever so slightly toward the left. It sounds preposterous, but she couldn't even talk about serving *leftovers* because the very word bothered him. Nor did she dare place any of the silverware on the left side of the plates because it disturbed him so. Fannie had to restrain herself from telling him he had gone so far right he was in left field!

Lem's obsession with rightist causes and his abhorrence of anything even slightly left of center got so bad the strangest thing happened. One morning he woke up unable to use his left hand. It just shriveled up. "It's useless!" he cried to Fannie as he dangled the hand in front of her. "Fannie, what am I going to do?"

Far Right

"Go and get your head examined, Lem," Fannie said dispassionately.

"My head? Why my head? It's my hand that's shriveled," Lem said frantically, cradling his left hand in his right.

"Oh yeh?" Fannie continued calmly. "I have news for you. Your—"

She wanted to tell him his brain had shriveled up, but she held back. "Your best bet is to contact Dr. Smucker. Let him take a look at it, Lem."

"Dr. Smucker!" Lem blurted. Arching his right eyebrow, he continued disdainfully, "Dr. Smucker lives on the Left Bank. You can't expect me to go there!"

Fannie glowered. "Do you want help or don't you?"

So Lem went to Dr. Smucker, and he went to many more doctors in the weeks and months that followed. Why? Because neither Dr. Smucker nor any of the other doctors had the right answer to explain what had happened.

"No right answer?" Lem asked incredulously. "But there has to be a right answer. Right! Right! Right! There is only one answer and it's right, absolutely far right," he preached to a startled Dr. Smucker. However, try as he would, in the months that followed Lem was unable to find the right answer. Instead, he was given a variety of opinions.

"It could be housemaid's knee," Dr. Linkeputz solemnly proposed.

"In my hand?" Lem asked in amazement.

"It's been known to travel," the doctor added sagely.

"Too much wrist action in breaking eggs. I see it all the time," another doctor nodded knowingly.

"But I haven't got the problem in my right wrist," Lem puzzled.

"It's a left-wristed problem," the doctor stated curtly. Other doctors had other pronouncements that frequently contradicted the others.

"Too little calcium in the bone."

"Too much calcium in the bone."

"Not the right kind of calcium in the bone."

Since previously Lem had always had an answer for everything (and the right one at that), having no answer was quite an education for him. There had never been an uncertainty in his life before, and consequently there had never been room for discussion or debate. But now everything had changed.

As the weeks and months passed, his friends noticed Lem becoming less dogmatic and inflexible on issues that previously he had approached so rigidly. He listened sympathetically to his children at the dinner table as they gradually revealed more and more of their own uncertainties on different issues. One evening before Lem went to the synagogue, Fannie gasped as Lem told his youngest child, "There are no easy answers. Sometimes we are left to live in the dark and wait. I cannot tell you the answer to your question." Looking at his left hand resting limp on the table he added, "Perhaps you will just have to make friends with your question and be gentle to it." Then he caressed his hand for a minute, got up, kissed Fannie good-bye, and left for the synagogue.

Lem entered the synagogue and sat down on a bench near the front. Closing his eyes, he prayed silently for about fifteen minutes before he was distracted by murmuring nearby. Lem tried to ignore it, but the murmuring erupted into an argument. A young man

Far Right

in his thirties was standing in the front with three officials of the synagogue. He recognized the officials as men whom he had once greatly admired because they too believed in a hard-headed approach to interpreting the law. Now, however, their approach seemed distant and harsh to Lem. As for the young man, he didn't know him personally, but he had seen him in the synagogue more than once. Lem's friends spoke warmly of his compassion. "Jesus, that's his name," Lem muttered as he tuned in to the heated discussion.

"Is it lawful to work a cure on the Sabbath?" one of the officials angrily demanded of Jesus.

"Hmmmm, I would have had a quick answer to that a year ago," Lem thought as he nodded his head.

Jesus lost no time firing back. "Suppose one of you has a sheep and it falls into a pit on the Sabbath. Will you not take hold of it and pull it out? Well, think how much more precious a human being is than a sheep. Clearly, good deeds may be performed on the Sabbath."

Lem was so intrigued by the discussion that he had gotten up and advanced to where the men were arguing. Jesus noticed him, stopped what he was saying for a moment and then continued slowly, "Stretch out your left hand." At first Lem thought Jesus was addressing someone else, but as Jesus continued looking straight at him it became clear Jesus meant Lem. To his own surprise, Lem found himself extending his hand to Jesus. Jesus took Lem's hand and, covering it with his own hands, gently massaged it. Lem felt a surge of strength in the hand and began wiggling his fingers for the first time in months.

Filled with awe and gratitude, Lem spoke from his heart. "Thank you. Thank you very much, sir."

SETUPS

Jesus smiled as he commented, "Perhaps now the left and the right can help one another. There's no need for one to be more dominant than the other." Then, looking directly into Lem's eyes, he added slowly, "Is there?" At first Lem didn't understand, but then he slowly nodded his head as he realized what Jesus meant. He brought his hands together in quiet repose; Lem was finally at peace with himself.

Reflection

*I'm really somebody
because I have a corner on salvation.*

We can become so caught up in a religious adherence to an ideology that we have no time left for God or anyone else. Our ideologies are our salvation. Not that we necessarily live and die by religious formulae, but we adhere religiously to certain propositions or illusions in such a way that everything else takes second place. In "Tripped Up," Sol swore by the Law, the Law that he identified with God. If this Law were violated, then he became outraged because he saw the Law as God. This is not so different from believing that saying the Pledge of Allegiance and waving the flag is being patriotic. We consider worthy of our righteous indignation anyone not mouthing the words or going through the motions. To hell with the fact that these "commies" may be sheltering and feeding the homeless or doing a thousand and one other good things!

"The ticket for getting into the kingdom is knowing how to play," Jesus tells his disciples in "The Kingdom." They, too, are taken with a particular version of the kingdom as a very serious place to be. Presumably, those who enter have been saved from frivolity!

The wisdom of play allows us to laugh or be serious without literalizing what we are doing. We pretend Richard Burton is Hamlet and we discover something about this character Hamlet, but we also know Richard Burton is not Hamlet. Were Richard Burton to think "I am Hamlet" or we to make this identification, we would be like those who failed to distinguish word and image from what they are meant to express.

Being able to play is akin to taking our images of the holy seriously, but not so seriously that we identify one with the other.

Jesus always says the kingdom is "like...," not "is...." By the same token, we might do better to say Jesus is "like...," not Jesus "is...," because whether we are speaking of the kingdom or Jesus we are referring to *our* words and *our* images about the holy. They will always prove inadequate for expressing what is ultimately unimaginable and unutterable. This being the case, it is preposterous to claim we have a corner on salvation because we subscribe to a particular dogma, creed, or ritual. Not only do we *not* have a grip on salvation, we increasingly lose our grip on reality.

We can become so devoted to an ideology that we lose connection with our lives in the here and now. Fascination with ideologies that lift us off our feet and carry us away is Lem's problem in "Far Right." For Lem, as for many people like him, the word "right" is a manifestation of good. Words associated with "left" (like "leftovers") are the powers and principalities that frighten and intimidate Lem at every turn. "Preposterous!" we say. Not if we pay attention to the way words like "liberal" and "conservative" conjure up good or evil depending which side of the aisle we happen to be on.

Left-wing or right-wing causes draw the allegiance and fervor of supporters that put to shame the average parishioner's allegiance to his or her church. Whoever and whatever other people are really like is lost once we've labeled them "right" or "left." Their religious affiliation makes them either saints or sinners who need to be either exalted or exorcised. They represent all that is good and clean or all that is bad and dirty. Such is our enchantment under an ideology such as Lem's.

What kind of an attachment do we bring to our belief systems, our causes, and our projects? Are we threatened by other ways of believing, and do we think our formulation of what we believe can never be questioned? In other words, has the holy been reduced to being nothing more than a recipe? Have we based our being somebody on having a corner on salvation?

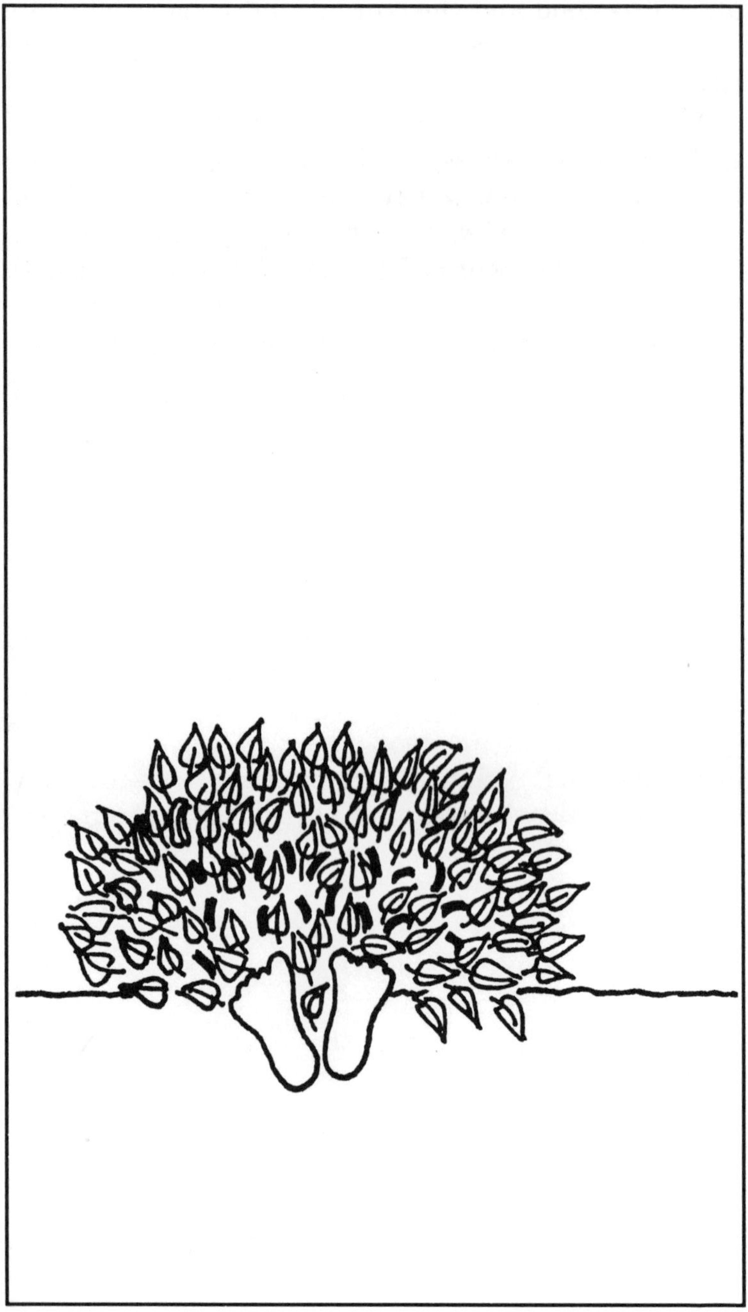

WHERE ARE YOU?

Luke 16:19-20: "Once there was a rich man who dressed in purple and linen and feasted splendidly every day. At his gate lay a beggar named Lazarus who was covered with sores."

"He knows how to dress. Look at those tunics! Gold embroidered. Designer made," boasted the butler to the chef.

"Knows how to eat too," the chef responded, his high chef's hat bobbing approvingly. "Crepes and powdered strawberries for breakfast; asparagus spears and lamb chops for lunch; beef tenderloin a la roche in the evening and..."

"But have you seen his wine cellar?" his steward interrupted. "Vintage chablis, roses, zinfandels, and mozels from all over the world."

Standing in the kitchen of the large, white-pillared mansion, they all agreed: Dives, their employer, had taste. He was *au courant* regarding what was fashionable and chic. But it didn't end there. He was also socially aware.

SETUPS

"Bring me the *Jerusalem Post, Herald, Times,* and the *Jericho News!* I like to keep abreast of all the world's problems, how they developed over night, and what the latest suggestions are for solving them."

His butler was routinely impressed as he ran to fetch the newspapers. "You know, the Master is deeply concerned about you people," he informed the poor man lying disheveled on the large front porch.

"Oh, really?" the scraggly bearded man answered feebly. "Glad to hear it. Maybe he could give me some bread for me and my buddies," he pleaded.

Ignoring his plea, the butler continued, "By the way, don't lie in the way of those newspapers when they're thrown on the porch. You could get hurt you know."

"Oh yeh, yeh," the old man mumbled as he dragged his body off the porch.

"Butler! Butler!" Dives called from within.

"Yes, Master?" the butler cocked an ear towards the mansion.

"Have the lawyers from the Civil Liberties Union arrived yet?"

"Not yet, sir!"

"Oh! Let me know as soon as they get here."

"Yes sir," the butler answered. Smiling benignly at the old man, the butler launched into another round. "See, he has a heart of gold. Wants to make certain nobody's rights are denied, especially junkies, muggers, and neo-nuts. What I really like is that he leaves no stone unturned to help whoever's under it. Isn't that great?" the butler chortled as he nudged the old man with his foot as you would a tired hound.

Where Are You?

"Yeh, yeh, mighty helpful man, your boss! Like to meet him some day. Do you think he's got an extra shirt or pair of shoes he could throw my way? Or something for my buddies?"

Once more the butler ignored the old man's request. "Oh, perhaps you will meet him. My master steps onto the porch every morning to enjoy the view. Maybe you'll be lucky enough to see him." The butler continued in a hushed conspiratorial voice, "But do you think you could crawl into that bush over there? Nothing personal, you understand, but it would require a little effort stepping over your body to get onto the porch and enjoy the view. Wouldn't want you to get hurt now, would we?"

"Sure, sure! I understand," the old man agreed, and he inched painfully into a large, green sticker bush off to the side of the porch. Once there the only signs of his presence were his labored breathing and the soles of his bare feet reflecting through the bush.

"Butler! Butler!"

"Yes, Master? What can I do, do, do for you?"

"My priest is supposed to be here at two this afternoon for a personal prayer service. I'd like the patio readied."

"Yes, yes, Master. Consider it done," the butler called back, doing a little jig on the concrete walk. Then, directing his attention to the bush, he jabbered enthusiastically, "Did you know my master has his own personal priest come and pray to his own personal Lord and Savior for his own personal needs once a week? What a personal privilege to serve such a master's personal whims. I'm just ecstatic!" The servant waltzed around the bush, got down on all fours, tickled the feet of the old man, and cried, "Aren't you happy?"

"Oh, oh," the old man groaned. The unexpected tickle had startled him so that he cut himself on the stickers. "My feet hurt. Has your boss got any salve or Band-Aids? Anything at all to relieve the pain?"

Not listening, the butler spoke directly to the man's soles, "Would you consider it an inconvenience to pull your feet into the bush just a little bit more?"

"Oh no, no," the old man muttered. Slowly, painfully, the feet disappeared.

"That's better, much better." The butler rose and was about to turn away when he just couldn't help asking one last thing. "Ah, if you can manage it, could you hold your breath? Sounds like some kind of rattle in your throat. We wouldn't want people to think there was a snake in the bushes, now would we?" He waited for an answer but there was none, nor was there any more heavy breathing. Indeed, no breathing at all. "Well you certainly are obliging," the butler said admiringly. He took a long, hard look at the bush, surveyed the yard, and seeing that all was well, he cleared his throat, shaped his hands like a megaphone, and yelled, "Master! You can come out now. Everything looks great!"

Within seconds the front door opened and Dives stepped out onto his porch. "You're right," he said. "Everything looks great. I see no one with problems. No one at all!" No sooner had he spoken, however, than he tripped on the hem of his long purple tunic (long tunics were all the rage that year), fell forward off the porch, hit his head on the concrete walk, and suffered a fatal concussion. He died that day.

Where Are You?

Next thing Dives knew, he woke up on someone's very, very hot front porch. His throat was dry as dry could be, so he moaned, "Oh, oh. Does anybody have a glass of Perriere handy?"

"Perriere? Did someone ring for Perriere?" a voice from within asked.

"Yes, yes. Here! I'll even settle for La Croix. Tap water if necessary. Anything really!"

A huge, bald-headed man with a beard and a large gold earring and a tall glass of ice water emerged from a mansion that uncannily resembled Dives' own white-pillared mansion. "Where are you?" the man called as he brought his hand to his forehead and strained to see Dives. "I can't see you."

"I'm here, here in front of you! You'll trip over me if you get any closer!"

The man took a step forward and walked right through Dives' bulky body without knowing it. "Where are you? In the bushes?" the man asked.

"I'm—" Dives was going to repeat himself, but seeing it wouldn't help, he muttered, "Forget it!"

"Sorry, wherever you are," the man apologized, "but the visibility is unusually bad. Seems like the previous owner created that kind of climate. I wish it were different but, there's not much I can do about that."

"Is there anyone else you'd be able to get in touch with, say, my brothers?" Dives pleaded. "Warn them against creating this invisibility problem!"

"Maybe the old fellow inside can help you," he nodded toward the mansion. Cupping his hand around his mouth, he shouted, "Lazarus! Can you hear me?" There was no answer. Again he cried, "Lazarus! Can you hear me?"

"Barely," a voice within answered almost inaudibly.

"There's someone out here who needs your help," the big man explained. "Can you come to the door?"

"I'd like to but there are so many people partying in here with Abe, it's impossible to get even near the door," the voice replied. "Sorry about that. I'll do what I can once the party is over, but there's a rumor going around that it's going to last a long time."

The big guy shrugged his shoulders. "You heard him, buddy! I can't see you and he can't get to you. I bet you've had that problem too!"

Dives shook his head sadly. He had the problem all right. But he saw it from both sides now!

Reflection

I'm really somebody because I talk a good game.

It is remarkable how we can so easily mistake our rhetoric about concern for others as actual concern. Perhaps it helps us feel better about ourselves and perpetuates the illusion that if we talk a good game, we really are good! *Abracadabra!* and the word creates the reality!

Feeling overwhelmed by the presence of so much injustice, we often attempt to remedy our helplessness with meetings, discussions, dialogues, and conferences dealing with social issues. In "Where Are You?" Dives lived with the illusion that reading and discussing social issues is acting responsibly toward the poor and the homeless. The butler conspired to keep that illusion alive by keeping the front porch and lawn clear of anyone whose presence might challenge the illusion.

Dives' sin was not that he saw and ignored but that he didn't want to see and consequently be faced with the decision to act on what he saw.

What don't we want to see? What do we go out of our way to avoid seeing? How do we deal with our own feeling of being helpless in the presence of injustice or evil? Do we in any way live with the illusion that we are somebody because we talk a good game?

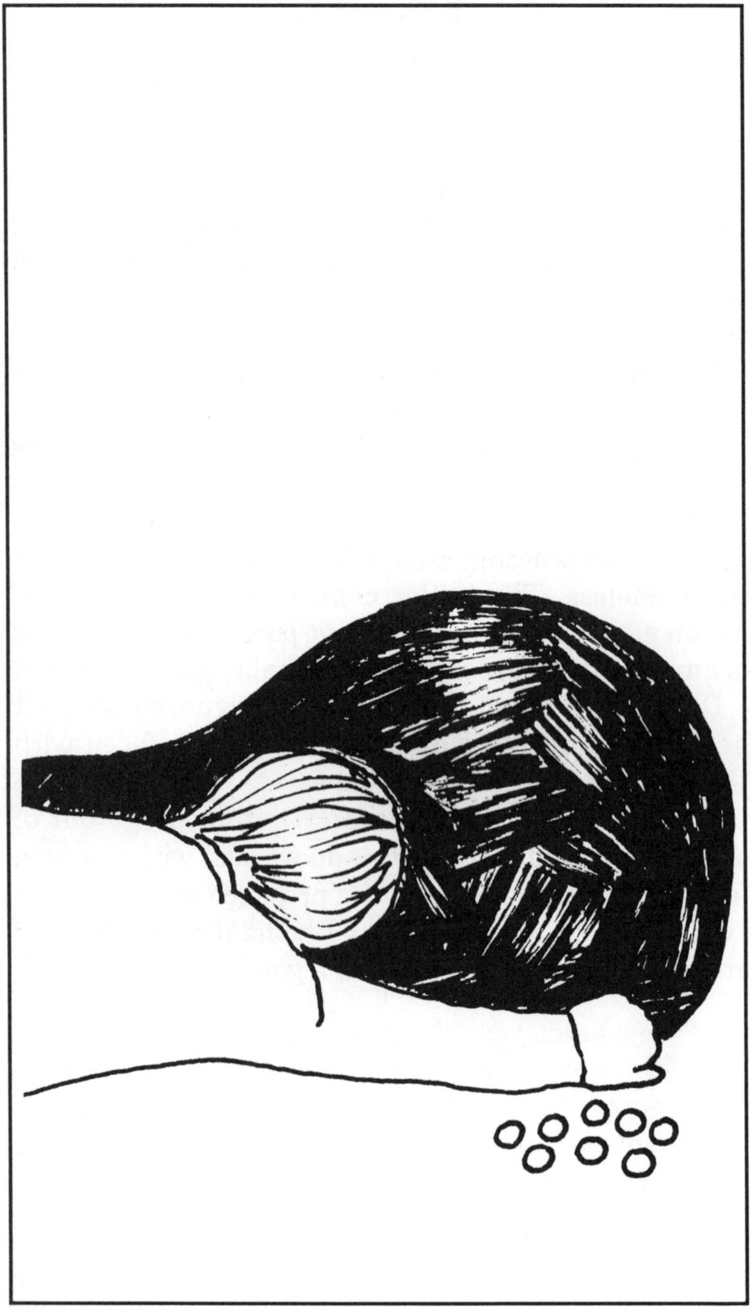

JUDAS

Matthew 26:14-16: Then one of the Twelve whose name was Judas Iscariot went off to the chief priests and said, "What are you willing to give me if I hand him over to you?" They paid him thirty pieces of silver, and from that time on he kept looking for an opportunity to hand him over.

"Who'll volunteer time to gather secondhand clothing for the needy in Jericho?"

"I'll do it! Judas is the name."

"Who'll run errands for the elderly in Jericho's shantytown?"

"I'll do it! Judas is the name."

"Who'll deliver speeches on behalf of the homeless kids in Jericho?"

"I'll do it! Judas is the name."

If anyone needed help, Judas Iscariot invariably offered his services—provided, of course, that those in need were truly poor. Not simply the elderly or the emotionally disturbed or the disabled, but only the really poor among them got Judas' help. Never ever the affluent! God forbid that Judas have any association with the fat cats of the city!

SETUPS

So when the young man from Nazareth came to Jericho one day preaching passionately about God's special love of the poor, Judas cocked an ear and listened intently. Fascinated by the compassionate message, Judas was convinced this was the man he wanted to follow. "Surely," he thought, "he will champion the cause of the poor and right the wrongs they endure. With his help, there is nothing we can't do!"

"Master, I want to follow you," he begged Jesus.

"Take him on," Jesus' friends urged. "His zeal is commendable."

"He won't let you down," boasted Judas' associates.

"He's done more for the poor in Jericho than anyone else!"

Declaring fervently, "I'm committed to the cause," Judas confessed, "And I've known poverty myself. My folks slaved all their lives for the rich of Jericho. It's no fun being poor."

Having listened carefully, Jesus was uneasy but under pressure, so he relented. "Judas is excessive in his zeal and his talk about the 'cause,' but he has heart," Jesus thought. "Surely time will temper him," he hoped.

But the passage of time only intensified Judas' zeal. "I was embarrassed the other day when we walked down the street and Jesus stopped one of those fat-bellied burghers to ask him about his sick wife," Judas noted angrily to a friend. "Imagine that! Concerned about the health of a woman who probably wouldn't think twice if one of her own servants were dying!" Judas didn't wait for any reaction but launched into another attack. "And talk about ogling the hookers! What else could he be doing when he strolls over and strikes up conversations with them? Flirting! Wasting time on them when he could be organizing the poor to battle for their rights!"

"He has no regard for the poor, then?" his friend puzzled.

"No regard? That's not the point!" Judas dismissed the question. "He's muddying the waters by inviting everybody, and I mean every-body, to listen to his message. It's not fair!" he cried, as if Jesus had hurt him personally. "God is a God of the poor—no more, no less! Why does Jesus traffic with the rich? Dine at their tables? Sip their expensive wines? Exchange pleasantries with oppressors?" Looking furtively around, he continued in a hushed voice, "Just yesterday he interrupted time I needed with him for this rich kid who couldn't make up his mind what to do with his life. Ha! Luxury problems! That the poor should all have the luxury of frittering away their lives!"

Pointing in the direction of a distant crowd, he pressed his grievance further. "And even now he's swapping stories with those tax collectors who leech the blood from the poor. I tell you, I don't know what's happened to Jesus! When I met him, I saw promise in his message—potential for programs to wipe out poverty and oppression! Endless possibilities! But now there's no focus, no practical point to his preaching. Instead we have this prattle about love and God's rule—a smoke screen for doing nothing! Permission to hobnob with tax collectors and whores and with all the losers who come along." Judas paused and added sarcastically, "No discrimination whatsoever! He wants it both ways, but he can't have it!"

"So why do you continue to stay on with him?" his friend wondered.

Judas hesitated. "I'm not sure. He still fascinates me. There's something in his manner: a simplicity, a trustworthiness that is disarming," he mused, his voice softer, gentler than it had been during the entire conversation. Then, stroking his beard, he chuckled, "And every now and then Jesus' anger gets the better of him and he lets the right people have it right between the eyes! Like the day he gave it to the merchants in the Temple. Whip in hand, he sent them scurrying into every corner. It's times like that when I see the Jesus who draws me on. In those moments I think there's still a possibility to get him moving on the right track." Judas added resentfully, "The direction we were supposed to be on from the beginning." Finally, slowly and ominously, he concluded, "I don't know what I'd do at this point if he did something else with which I strongly disagreed."

Two days later Judas discovered what he would do. Jesus and a small group of his friends including Judas were invited to a get-together at Simon the leper's house. While they were eating, a woman entered the room. She held an expensive jar of perfume. Seeing Jesus, she walked over to him and, as a gesture of affection and respect, poured the perfume over his head. Immediately the guests, including Jesus's disciples, began to argue.

"What is the point of this extravagance? This perfume could have been sold for a good price and the money given to the poor," Judas stormed.

But Jesus defended her action. "Why do you criticize the woman? What she did was good." Looking right at Judas he said pointedly, "The poor you will always have with you, but you won't always have me. In doing this she has actually contributed toward preparing my burial."

Judas said nothing. He was obviously angered and hurt by what he perceived to be an injustice against the very people Jesus claimed to help. But deep inside he felt betrayed. Jesus had berated him in public. Excusing himself, he had barely gotten out of the room when he erupted. "That's it! How could he? I cannot believe he would trivialize the poor that way. Letting some silly woman waste one hundred dollars' worth of perfume by dribbling it on his head. Denying the poor by wasting it on himself! And what's his excuse? Contributed toward his burial! Well, two can play that game! As far as I'm concerned, he's betrayed the poor. He's let them down! He's let me down! I'll make him pay back what rightfully belongs to the poor, with interest!"

"What will you give me for him?" he had asked the chief priests. When they had given him thirty silver pieces and left, he held the coins high and reveled, "Well, Jesus, I hope you're still enjoying the perfume because you've paid for it now! This will go to the poor! And you, you will go..." Judas' voice weakened, "Go where? With them, with those rich..." Judas couldn't prevent the truth of what he had done from dawning. He slumped to the ground, stunned by the enormity of what he had done.

"But this is different. I'm different," he argued with himself. "I love the poor. I'm not doing this for me! I'm clean, I'm focused, I'm committed to the one cause that really counts." His voice grew more desperate. "But Jesus, he's..., well he's not tough, not decisive. He doesn't, couldn't really love the poor, love me, give us what we really need. He's betrayed us by going over to them, loving them. He's betrayed—" The words stuck in his throat. He couldn't utter them with any conviction. "How could he dare to love them!" And rising slowly, his eyes fixed, he whispered, "And how could I have betrayed him? Oh, God, there's some mistake here. Maybe it's not too late." And he ran off frantic to undo the evil he had done for love of the poor.

Reflection

*I'm really somebody
because you're my everything.*

When we speak of infatuation, we ordinarily think of a relationship between the sexes, but infatuation also exists between members of the same sex, as in hero worship. The other becomes the center of one's life: the one who will save the day. The illusion created in infatuation is that we are really somebody because of our association with a special "other" who has become everything to us. Judas, infatuated with his hero, Jesus, is one such person.

Initially Judas is enchanted by Jesus and his message to the poor. From the start, his zeal for the "cause" disturbs Jesus, and from our introduction's discussion of the setup, we can appreciate his concern. After all, Judas was in search of an idol: someone whom he could idealize and who could meet his own deepest, unacknowledged needs. But what he couldn't accept was who Jesus really was and what Jesus himself needed to be. When we speak of an infatuated person setting himself up for a big letdown, Judas comes to mind.

The big letdown resulted in Judas' feeling betrayed. In turn he lashes out at Jesus for betraying the interests of the poor in favor of the rich, for "oggling" the prostitutes, etc. Unable to recognize how much attention he himself demanded from Jesus, he condemned Jesus for ignoring *their* needs. Now Judas was projecting his own unacknowledged shadow side onto Jesus, his own capacity to vacillate and betray. And because he was oblivious to this, he could rationalize going to the priests and selling Jesus out "on behalf of the poor."

The dawning insight into his own treachery was too much for him, and consequently he was overwhelmed. His inability to accept his own demon exemplifies how the whole process of idolizing, demonizing, and humanizing can be aborted.

The awareness and integration of our shadow is an essential life task, and if we deny the shadow we become the zealots, fanatics, super-patriots, and extremists who divide the world into opposing camps: the forces of light, among whom we number ourselves, and the forces of darkness. In this unhappy situation, we then attempt to condemn, attack, ban, and destroy the intolerable evil we see in others, without being the least aware that so much of what we hate in them springs from within us.

Who have been the heroes or heroines in our lives? Whom have we idolized and imitated? What did we expect from them—direction or meaning in life? And are they still our heroes, or have they fallen off their pedestals? How do we regard them now? With anger? Sadness? What did our expectations of them tell us about ourselves? Did we nurse the illusion that we were really someone because the other was everything to us?

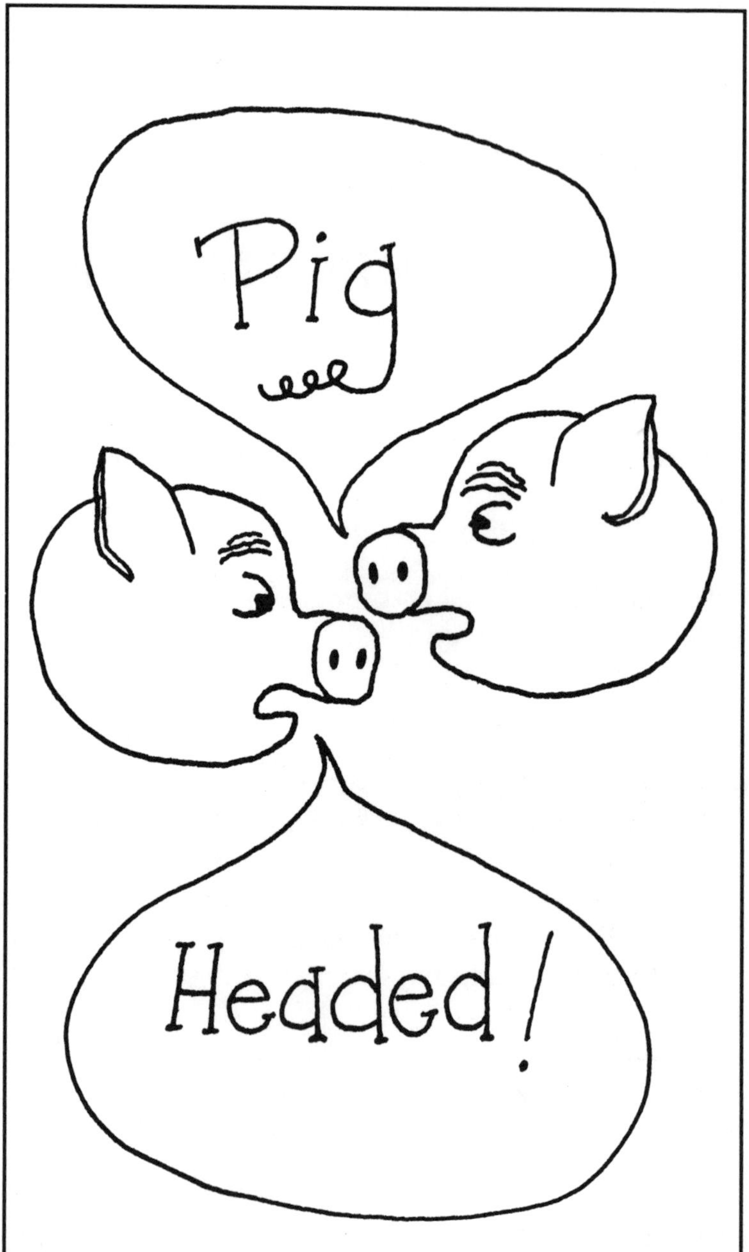
Pig
Headed!

PIG-HEADED

Matthew 8:30-32 Some distance away a large herd of swine was feeding. The demons kept appealing to him, "If you expel us, send us into the herd of swine."

"Peanut butter goes better on white bread!"
"No, it's better on rye!"
"Walking is healthier than running!"
"No, running is healthier than walking."
"You go up to Jerusalem but down to Jericho."
"No, you go down to Jerusalem and up to Jericho."
"Sopranos are paid more than altos."
"No, altos are paid more than sopranos."

On and on they went. They never agreed with one another. Each insisted he was right. Both got so worked up they had to spend one or two days in bed before their blood pressure would stabilize. The only characteristic they shared in common was their pig-headedness! Two unyielding, pig-headed old men, who for some pig-headed reason insisted on living next-door to one another.

"Merv, why don't you relax on the front porch when Irv is sitting on his back porch," his wife, Myra, urged.

SETUPS

"No, I'll sit when and where I want," Merv grumbled as he shook his fist in the direction of his neighbor's house.

"Irv, doesn't it make sense to work the garden on Wednesday mornings instead of Tuesdays when Merv is working his?" Irv's wife, Thelma, suggested.

"No, I'll work when and where I want," Irv insisted as he stuck out his tongue in the direction of Merv's house.

The truth is Merv and Irv needed one another, although neither would ever admit this to anyone! Not to their wives, not to one another, and certainly not to themselves. But still, the truth was they needed each other as foils. Neither Irv's nor Merv's families, friends, or associates came close to doing for them what they, in a perverse kind of way, were doing for one another.

This strange relationship exploded one day when the two combatants took up their battle stations. Each knew the other's schedule perfectly. So at exactly one in the afternoon each opened his own back door, strolled out onto his own back porch, and sat down on his own swing, one facing the other. An uneasy silence prevailed. Then Merv fired the opening volley by ostensibly addressing his remarks to Myra inside the house but actually intending them for Irv.

"Myra, the Jericho tomatoes I planted are a lot more tasty than those Jerusalem tomatoes some people I know have planted."

Irv reared his head like an old war horse. "Thelma, thank God we've got Class A Jerusalem tomatoes in our garden, not that junk from Jericho."

Pig-Headed

"Myra," Merv shot back, "Did I ever tell you that people who plant Jerusalems know nothing about gardening?"

"Thelma," Irv laughed sarcastically, "do you know what farmers call people who plant Jerichos? The Jericho Jerks! Ha! Ha!"

"Pea brain!" Merv growled directly at Irv.

"Rattle head," Irv reciprocated.

Both men rose, walked ominously to the edges of their porches, and glared at one another.

"Bull head!" Merv grunted.

"Fruitcake!" Irv spat back.

"Turkey poop!" Merv had hit an all time low.

"Mouse turd!" Ditto for Irv.

They had argued from their porches every day for years like this. After an hour or so they'd always shake their fists at one another and retreat into their respective houses. But today the arguing didn't subside after an hour. It escalated into a sensational and totally irrational display of pig-headedness. Their wives and children pleaded with Merv and Irv to stop; but they didn't. Friends and relatives came over to persuade them to call it a day; but the two ignored their attempts. Finally, near dusk, the local rabbi visited and what he witnessed convinced him that the two did not stop because they could not stop.

"They're possessed by some alien power," he announced, yelling to be heard over the din. "There is nothing I can do." There was nothing anyone could do; and so two days and hundreds of complaints later, the city officials banished Merv and Irv to the outskirts of the city in a place called the Tombs: a place where the possessed spent their days and nights.

SETUPS

Although Merv and Irv were chained to the walls of different dreary tombs, they were still within shouting distance of one another. Four or five times a day and often during the night, they'd routinely pound the walls and howl at one another for hours. Then, they'd sleep from sheer exhaustion. This went on for five years.

Into this situation came a young rabbi, Jesus of Nazareth. He had visited tombs like these on more than one occasion and consequently was acquainted with the terrible variety of their inmates. He knew very well how needy every person was and the demonic behavior such neediness sometimes generated.

As much out of curiosity at their relatives' description of them as out of compassion, Jesus walked toward the tombs with his friend Peter that day. Standing outside the cave of first one, then the other, Jesus and Peter eavesdropped on their harangue. Peter was distressed to see Jesus mimic their antics. "Why are you doing that, Jesus?" he scolded. "Do you want to become like them?"

"Perhaps," Jesus answered enigmatically. "Perhaps." Scratching his head, Peter wondered what Jesus was up to. He was soon to find out.

Once Merv and Irv had fallen off to sleep, Jesus positioned himself close to the entrance of one cave and tossed a stone into it.

"Wha—? What?" Merv was startled awake and rattled the chains that held him fast.

"It's me. Irv," Jesus answered mimicking Irv's voice. "Who else would it be?"

Merv wasted no time in taking the offensive. "Your Jerusalem tomatoes suck!"

"My Jerusalem tomatoes do suck!" Jesus agreed.

Pig-Headed

Thinking he hadn't been heard, Merv repeated all the louder, "I said, 'Your Jerusalem tomatoes suck!'"

"I know it," Jesus answered.

"You're a nerd!"

"I am a nerd!"

Merv didn't know what to make of this. Whatever he shouted, the voice agreed. "I'm smart!"

"You are."

"I'm smarter than you."

"You are smarter."

"I know more about gardening than you."

"I know you do. You're an excellent gardener."

Not only did "Irv" agree with everything, but he agreed in such a way as to make Merv feel good. By the time the exchange ended an hour later, Merv found himself repeating his initial outburst, but with a difference. "Your Jerusalem tomatoes aren't always that bad!"

"You're right," the voice answered. Merv said nothing. He just sat perfectly still reveling in a newfound peace. Meanwhile Jesus had gone over to the entrance of Irv's cave, threw in a stone, woke Irv, and proceeded to do exactly what he had done with Merv. The results were the same.

Jesus retreated and waited with Peter for the two to resume what ordinarily would have been an outburst of charge and countercharge.

"Merv, are you there?" Irv called out gently.

"Yeh, Irv, how are you?"

"Not bad, Merv. How about you?"

"OK, I guess."

"When do you think they'll let us out? I'd really like to go home and try some of your Jerusalem tomatoes," Irv suggested.

"Same here, Irv. Maybe we can get together and share what we have with one another," Merv said amiably.

"Probably make a great spaghetti sauce!"

"Not a bad idea!"

"You know, I haven't felt this good in years," Merv sighed.

"Me, either," Irv agreed. "It's like something that has been with me for years is gone."

"Yeh."

Jesus listened, nodding approvingly. He looked off into the distance as he saw a herd of pigs racing headlong toward cliffs that overlooked the sea. "My, my, I'm glad our two friends changed the direction of their lives. Otherwise, more than pigs would have gone over the edge to certain destruction." Looking at Peter, he raised a finger, warning, "Peter, I think we better leave. I'm sure the neighbors are going to blame us for what has happened here today, and they will want us to leave."

And so the neighbors did. But not before Jesus had sought and gotten the release of Merv and Irv. They were free at last!

Reflection

I'm really somebody because I'm always right.

The need to be right may be a version of the need to be adequate. The more we can oppose others and prove them wrong, then the more right we are and our adequacy is established. However, a genuine sense of adequacy ought not depend on another's inadequacy. When it does, the false sense of adequacy soon vanishes and the cycle begins all over again. Once more, we need an other to put down so we can feel good about ourselves. The illusion, then, is that another's inadequacy is the only basis for our adequacy; it is addictive because while it promises adequacy, it only delivers fleeting satisfaction. In the long run, it is bogus and empty.

In "Pig-Headed," Merv and Irv experienced disillusionment gently as Jesus broke their destructive cycle by refusing to oppose their conflicting claims to infallibility. When he agreed with them, they experienced a self-affirmation independent of verbally abusing the other. Out of their newfound adequacy they could now freely affirm one another. Consequently their chains could no longer constrain them, nor were they forced to continue living in the tombs.

Do we have to have the last word in any discussion? Do we feel uneasy with people who don't think as we do? And therefore do we think it essential to "convert" them to our point of view? Do we think if we're not right on some issue, we are not right? If our sense of self is dependent on always being right, then we too live the illusion we are somebody because we are always right.

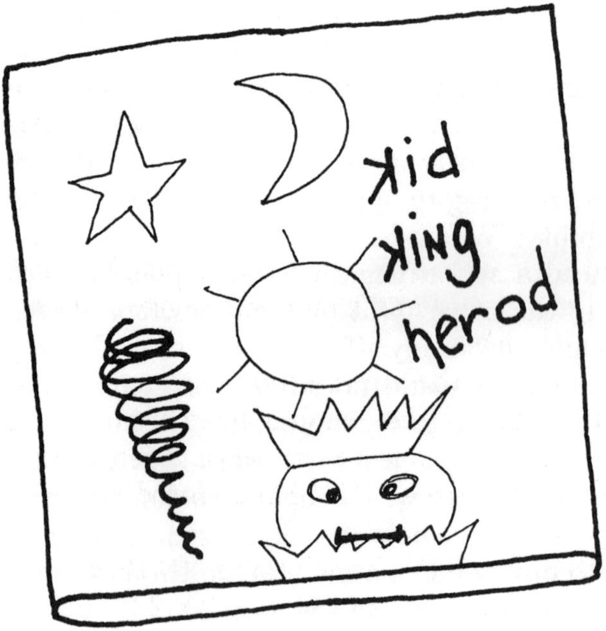
kid
king
herod

SUPERSTAR

Matthew 2:1-2: After Jesus' birth in Bethlehem of Judea during the reign of King Herod, astrologers from the east arrived one day in Jerusalem inquiring, "Where is the newborn king of the Jews? We observed his star at its rising and have come to pay him homage."

As far back as anyone could remember, Herod had to be the star.

"Our little Herod has the Midas touch. See how he's turned mere sand and water into a great castle," the queen chortled.

"Right!" All the court attendants agreed as they lined up to praise the formless heap of mud.

"Our little Herod is a math whiz, a genius actually. Wouldn't you agree?" Old King Herod demanded of his court mathematicians.

"Indeed! Indeed!" they chanted. Yet they wondered why all the fuss over multiplying 2 x 2.

"Herod's our darling, our dream, our rising star!" his parents boasted as they lifted high their ten year old for all the court to admire. "And he's your dream, your darling, too," they coaxed.

111

"By all means, by all means," everyone quickly concurred. Fingers crossed behind their backs, they loudly saluted him. "He's our dream, our darling, our rising star!"

Herod's parents vaunted him in every way. Not only was he a sand sculptor and a mathematics genius, in their estimation he was also a great painter as evidenced from his kindergarten doodles; a marvelous writer because he could string together a five-word sentence; a gifted dancer since he was able to jump up and down, especially when throwing temper tantrums. They also admired his assertiveness when he didn't get his own way, and the discipline he demonstrated in refusing to eat food he didn't deem appropriate to his princely status.

That he wasn't really the sculptor, mathematician, writer, painter, dancer, etc., they always declared him to be never crossed the doting couple's minds, even if it was an open secret in the court. As for little Herod, it was marvelously fun to be playing the rising star on centerstage.

"I'm the best! I'm the best!" the child prince chanted over and over while mom and dad looked on approvingly.

And when he was a young man, "I'm a prince of a fellow," he said admiringly as he swaggered from mirror to mirror in the 1,001 rooms of the palace.

There was one little hitch, however. For example, on one occasion the king said to little Herod, "You're a very courageous young man. You don't fear anybody or anything."

But Herod blurted, "No, no. Lots of people scare me!"

Superstar

"Don't talk that way!" his father snapped. "That wasn't you who said those words. The case is closed. Understood?" And Herod understood. He couldn't be afraid.

Or the time he told his mother, "Maybe others are as good at writing as I am."

The queen gasped, "Never, never. And don't let anyone tell you otherwise. If anyone claims or even appears to be better..." She hesitated, then continued ominously, "Well, you'll know what to do!"

Herod learned the lesson so well that when he ascended the throne there was clearly no room for any star in the kingdom but his own. That became particularly evident the day some astrologers brought him unexpected news.

"What? A star is born? In my kingdom? But that's impossible! It's centerstage for me and no one else. I'm the star around here!" Enraged, Herod wrung his hands and nervously paced the floor of the throne room. Royal ashtrays overflowed with half- smoked, king-sized cigarettes that filled the chambers with acrid smoke causing the frightened attendants' eyes to water. Stamping his red-slippered feet, he cried, "I won't have it! I won't have it!

"Attendant! Attendant! Where are you? Come here quickly!" A cowering adviser hurried to his side and prostrated himself on the floor. "What truth is there in the information from those star-struck astrologers?" he demanded, grinding his heel into the attendant's back.

"O Great Luminary of the Night," the adviser moaned, "it is true. Among the cavalcade of stars to appear in your kingdom, he is by far the brightest, the superstar who—"

113

"All right! All right!" Herod interrupted impatiently. "Cut the hype! Give me the facts. Where's this 'star' supposed to be born?"

"O Star Light, Star Bright, Brightest Star I've Seen This Night," fawned the attendant, "this new star is to be born in Bethlehem."

"Bethlehem, is it? Well, well, not exactly a showcase for stars, is it?" Herod sniffed. Thereupon he swung around, pounded repeatedly against the royal pillars and kicked it hard for good measure. "Ohhhh!" he groaned limping up his stairway to the stars. Sitting on the edge of the throne Herod massaged his royal kicker and ordered, "Send for those astrologers at once!"

When they arrived, Herod launched into a most egregious performance. Rising to his full height of 5'1", he danced lamely down the stairs and extended his arms, affecting a welcome any third-rate actor would have booed! "Gentlemen, gentlemen. We are delighted, de-lighted to hear about this new star on the horizon, this soup-, soup-, soup-..." Herod stammered, intimidated by the very thought of competition.

"Superstar," the attendant prompted.

"Yes, yes," Herod glared at the attendant. "We understand you wish to know from us where this star is to be born. Our scholars tell us the place is Bethlehem, a small, nondescript village. Certainly not the place I would have thought suitable for the birth of a soup-, soup-, soup-..."

"Superstar," the attendant whispered once more.

"A Superstart, er, Shooting Star, er, Superstar..." Herod continued. "Retired stars, stars gathering stardust, yes, maybe even a white dwarf star, but the origins of a Superstar, no!"

One of the astrologers, Balthasar, stepped forward and addressed Herod. "Your Excellency, we are grateful to you for telling us where we may find this star. We know nothing about the villages in your kingdom, but very soon we hope to discover for ourselves who this new star is."

"Marvelous, simply marvelous," Herod's smile contorted through his clenched teeth. Suddenly he lurched forward, having become dangerously tangled in his long, royal train. The three astrologers drew back instinctively from this wide-eyed specter barely in control of his pent-up rage.

"Phewww!" The court let out an audible sign of relief as Herod recovered his balance and continued in a vain attempt to soothe his visitors. "We are curious, nay, more than curious, extremely interested in meeting this star. Would you be so kind as to inform us exactly where we may offer this star our homage once you have found him?"

"By all means, Your Excellency," Caspar responded uncomfortably.

"Good! Good! Good!" Herod rubbed his hands together with relish. "I know you want to be on your way. So we shall not detain you further." Herod dismissed them with a royal flourish. Then, royally flushed, he muttered, "We'll see whose star is on the rise. As far as I'm concerned this is star wars!" He paused, then yelled, "Attendant!"

"Oh Wondrous King With Star-Crossed Eyes! I am here at your side!"

"Star-Crossed Eyes! Hmmmm..." Herod had to think about that one. "Attendant, let me know as soon as these astrologers come back. Once we get our royal hands on this kid we'll catch a falling star! Heh! Heh! Heh!" he laughed and elbowed the attendant. "Get it? Ever hear the tune?"

The attendant hadn't, but pretended and giggled, "Oh yes! Ha! Ha! Very funny!"

As the days passed into weeks, Herod's countenance and mood grew dark. He realized the astrologers would not make a return visit. He could no longer sleep or eat so fearful was he that there was someone better than himself in his kingdom. In the middle of the night, he'd search the nooks and crannies of the royal quarters for his phantom adversary. Often he shrieked into the dark corners, "I am the star, the only star!" He considered over and over what he could do to assure his stellar priority. One evening he recalled his mother's words that when anyone claimed to be better, he would know what to do. As he stood gazing out into the courtyard at one of the nurses holding his two-year-old son, his face hardened. "Yes, mother," he muttered, "I know what I shall do." Herod snapped his fingers and an attendant was immediately at his side.

"I want all of the boys of Bethlehem two years old and younger to be destroyed as soon as possible."

"Destroyed?" The attendant thought he had misunderstood.

"Yes, destroyed," Herod repeated.

"But, I..." the attendant's voice quavered.

"Do as I say!" Herod interrupted. "Or would you claim to know better than I?" The attendant immediately took his leave. Herod stood silently for a minute, then whispered, "There is only room for one superstar, and he alone will survive to be remembered."

Reflection

I'm really somebody because I'm number one.

Some people are always performing because they have been led to believe that being the star, darling, or center of attention is what makes them lovable. In "Superstar," Herod's problem was that as a child he had never been permitted to be anything less than a boy wonder. Not unlike many children, his reality was determined by his parents. He not only had to be onstage but on centerstage at all times—the little leaguer of Jerusalem! Herod had to suppress whatever feelings surfaced to contradict the posture of strength. The fragile self that all growing children share had to be disavowed and denied. He was number one and that was that!

The problem for Herod as king was that uncertainties and insecurities from a disavowed self kept popping up and threatening the only reality he accepted, that is, being the superstar. And the tragedy both for him and for the children he murdered was that along with the feelings of doubt and insecurity he repressed, he also lost contact with the only possible source of compassion and love in his life: the very self he had disowned.

Are we able to relax and not feel we need to be performing for others? Or do we feel compelled to excel, outdo, and prove ourselves number one in everything we do? Are feelings of tenderness as legitimate for us as feelings of competition and dominance? If we are in fact so compelled, then we are living the illusion we are somebody because we're number one.

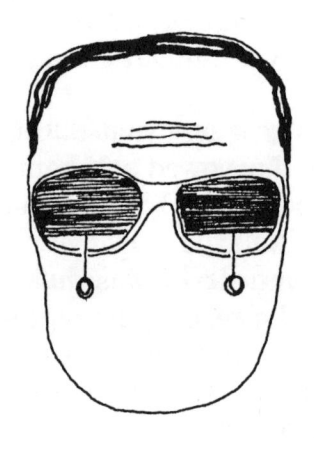

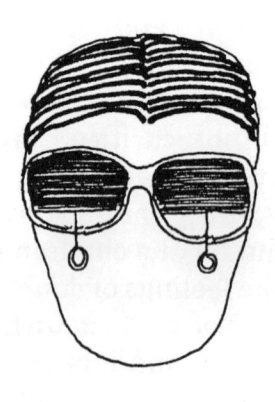

They would not believe
    in Jesus.

JOE'S BOY

Mark 6:5-6: Jesus could work no miracle there, apart from curing a few who were sick by laying hands on them, so much did their lack of faith distress him.

"Ohhh! I've got pains in my legs and pains in my arms. Do I need help!" Mrs. Minsky moaned.

"What was that?" Mr. Silberg put his hand to his ear, straining to catch Mrs. Minsky's latest complaint. "My hearing's bad. I need help or I'll be deaf in no time."

"Your hearing's bad? Can't be worse than my eye problem," Mrs. Terablum challenged. "Things are all blurred up for me. I'm black and blue running into so many doors!"

The three seniors were sitting at a table comparing aches and pains at the Nazareth Senior Center one hot afternoon. About thirty seniors congregated there every weekday.

"Selma Biddle over there has teeth problems," Mrs. Minsky confided in a hushed voice. "Seems they drop out every time she says hi or hello. It's terrible! Can't greet visitors properly so she makes up for it by yelling her good-byes."

"Tsk! Tsk! Don't tell me," Mrs. Terablum waved a hand. "I had the reverse problem a year ago. Every time I'd go to say good-bye, I could feel my uppers dropping. Folks I visited didn't know if I was mad at them or what when I'd just leave without saying good-bye."

"I guess half the people here could keep Dr. Smucker busy full-time," Mr. Silberg nodded. "Trouble is he's got his hands full with others in the town and we never get the help we need."

"Say," Mrs. Minsky interrupted, "who's the young fella that just came through the door? Nice looking!"

Jesus had just entered the day room and proceeded to strike up a conversation with three seniors seated nearest the door.

"I certainly don't know who he is," Mrs. Terablum chuckled. "I can hardly see what's in front of me."

"Whoever he is," Mr. Silberg observed, "he's helping Mrs. Lensky to her feet."

"Mrs. Lensky?" Mrs. Terablum sounded surprised. "It takes Mrs. Lensky forever and a day to get out of a chair. What did he do? Scare her?" she asked incredulously.

"No, no," Mrs. Minsky assured her. "He took her hand and brought her to her feet like she was light as a feather. She's got a smile on her face I haven't seen for years."

"And now he's gone to Mr. Blitzel's table." Mrs. Minsky was following Jesus' movement closely. "Of course Benny Blitzel can't see him on account of being so bent over. Now the young fellow is patting him on the back, and...oh my God..." Mrs. Minsky's eyes opened wide and she brought her hand to her mouth.

"What is it? What is it?" Mrs. Terablum asked excitedly.

"Mr. Blitzel is sitting up straight in his chair. Straighter than he was when there was nothing wrong with him."

By now all the seniors in the room had focused on Jesus and what he was doing. When Mr. Blitzel sat up straight, the seniors gave a round of applause. Then many of them crowded around Jesus buzzing and pointing to various aches that needed tending. Jesus ministered to them in turn; and each time he helped one senior, all the others applauded enthusiastically.

Finally, he came to the table where Mrs. Minsky, Mrs. Terablum, and Mr. Silberg sat. "Can I help you?" he asked.

"Oh yes! Why of course! Please do," they all answered.

Jesus placed his hands first on Mrs. Minsky's legs and arms, then on Mrs. Terablum's eyes, and finally on Mr. Silberg's ear. Within seconds all three of them noted a change.

"I can feel the ache leaving my legs and arms!" Mrs. Minsky squealed as she swung them freely for the first time in years.

"And I can hear you clear as a bell," Mr. Silberg rejoiced.

"I see you! I see you," Mrs. Terablum repeated over and over.

"We are grateful to you," Mrs. Minsky beamed. "We were just asking each other what your name is."

"Yes! Yes! What is your name?" Everybody in the room wanted to know.

"My name? My name is Jesus. I'm the son of Joseph and Mary. They live two blocks from here. My dad's a carpenter. I used to live here in town."

"You are Jesus?" Mrs. Terablum's voice registered disappointment as she sat down. "The carpenter's son? Oy, Mrs. Minsky, did you hear that? How can a carpenter's son do anything but put together boards?"

"And his mother? I've seen her take in the neighbor's wash. The neighbor's wash, mind you. How can anyone do what he did if his mother washed the neighbor's underwear? Especially *their* neighbor's underwear!" Mrs. Minsky spoke of Jesus as if he weren't standing there. Jesus remained silent.

"You don't get something from nothing," someone muttered.

"It's impossible that we should witness something so good coming from them. We know them," another added dogmatically.

"Right! That's right!" others chimed in. And as they did, a strange thing happened.

"I can't see you. I can't see you," Mrs. Terablum complained.

"My legs and arms hurt," Mrs. Minsky added.

"Eh? What did you say? What was that?" Mr. Silberg cocked an ear. And all around the room seniors who minutes earlier had experienced relief from aches and pains felt the pain return. Mr. Blitzel was bent over again and it took Mrs. Lensky forever to sit down.

Jesus watched all this sadly; there was nothing for him to do but silently slip away. When he had gone,

Mr. Silberg grumbled loudly enough for all to hear. "Of course I never really heard better! A lot of magic! That's all it was."

All the others added their two cents, including Mr. Blitzel. "I wasn't sitting up straight at all!"

"Let's say amen to that," they all agreed.

And Jesus could work no miracle there, apart from curing a few who were sick by laying hands on them, so much did their lack of faith distress him.

Reflection

I'm really somebody because we're in the know.

If we refuse or are unable to be dis-illusioned, it can be disastrous not only for ourselves but also for those affected by our illusion. An illusion can be described as a bias, an individual's or a goup's preferred way of understanding and responding to the world.

In "Joe's Boy" the bias or shared by the men and women at the Nazareth Senior Center, and the bias is this: What is extraordinary can't possibly come from the ordinary. Therefore, since Jesus is only the carpenter's son, and since his mother does the neighbor's wash, how could he possibly be a miracle worker?

Illusions, shared or not, can so constrain and straitjacket that if they don't accord with our experiences, we actually deny whatever we see, feel, hear, taste, and touch. Thus, in "Joe's Boy," prior to Jesus' disclosing his identity, he was able to heal the seniors of their ills. Their assumption of who could and couldn't heal was not yet operative. But as soon as he revealed himself as Joe's boy, the power of the illusion led them all to deny any healing had taken place.

Our own experience of meeting someone and having a great time with that person may be completely negated once we discover that the person is a Jew or an atheist or a homosexual. This is because of the shared assumptions or biasws we have about who or what kind of person she or he must "really" be. Then in retrospect we interpret negatively or positively why the person acted as he or she did. Here we can truly appreciate how our assumptions bind us and lead us further into self-bondage.

What are our shared assumptions about the people in our world? Are our standards of what is ugly or beautiful, proper or improper, right or wrong, good or bad, determined exclusively by what others think? Do we see others as they are or as they are filtered through the prism of "good ol' common sense?" If we do, are we still living with the illusion that we are somebody because we know the truth?

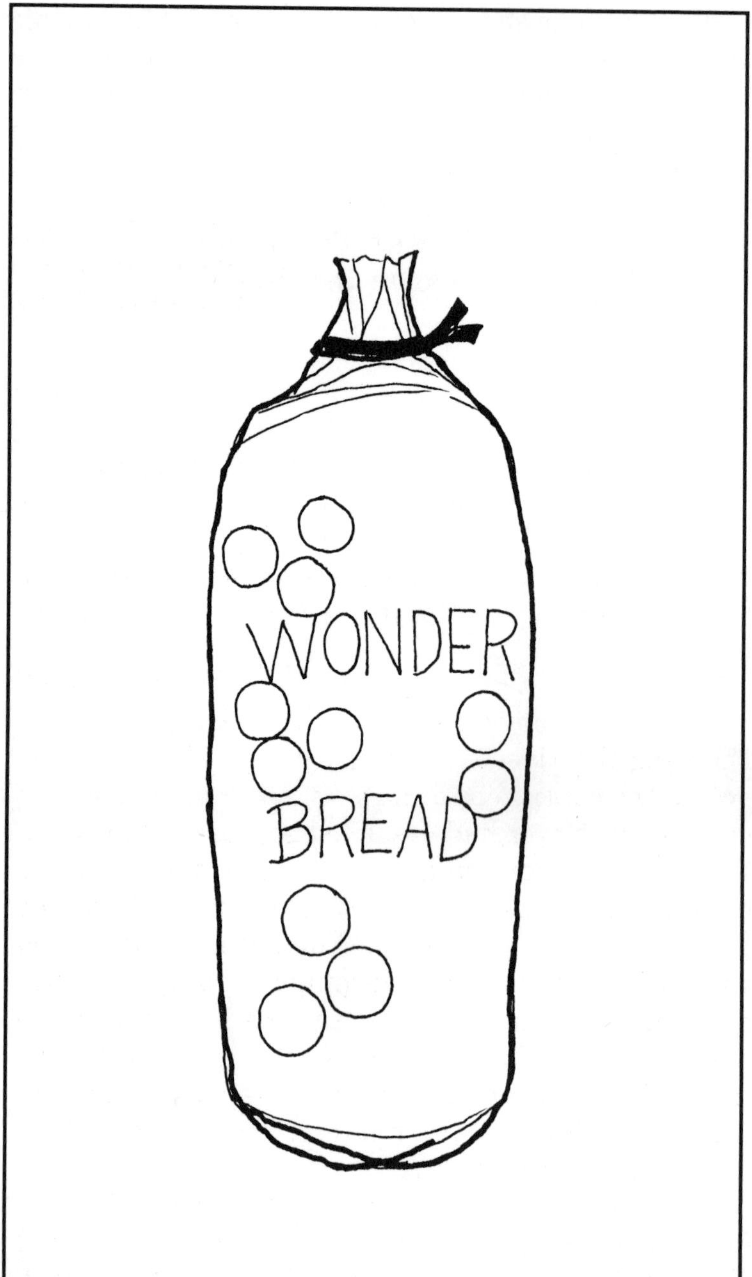
WONDER
BREAD

SPECIAL

Luke 4:1-3: Jesus, full of the Holy Spirit, then returned from the Jordan and was conducted by the Spirit into the desert for forty days, where he was tempted by the devil. During that time he ate nothing, and at the end of it he was hungry.

Was he a superstar at thirty? "Wow! I feel so good," he rejoiced as he staggered out of the Jordan River. Entering the river that afternoon, he had never expected the baptism by John would be such a profound experience. Never had Jesus felt so close to God as in those few precious minutes. "I know there are big plans in the works. I can feel it in my bones. His words are still ringing in my ears: 'You are my beloved; on you my favor rests!' This morning I felt so gloomy, but now that's all changed," he said as he scanned the desert from the Jordan's banks. "I've got to get away from this crowd and find out what his plans are. It just isn't clear what he's got in store. Yes, I've got to get away and sort this all out."

Into the desert Jesus strode, and there he fasted forty days and forty nights, waiting for some word about the big plans. Hungry but elated after the ordeal,

Jesus raised his hands to the sky and exclaimed, "Gee! I'm a little light-headed, but I've done it. Gone forty days without one bite of food!"

"Right on!" a voice rang out.

"Who's there?" Jesus spun around. He spied a kindly looking, little old man clothed in a white tunic, leaning against a boulder about ten feet away. "Right on!" he repeated.

"Where did you come from?" Jesus asked.

"Oh, I spend much of my time here, and I've seen lots of people try the kind of thing you've just done. But you're the first one to pull it off," he said admiringly.

"Really?" Jesus was flattered.

Walking slowly toward him, the man continued, "Of course I haven't paid attention to you every minute to be certain you didn't snack," he chuckled. "But then I didn't think it necessary because I knew you were special," he nodded gravely.

"No kidding!" Jesus' eyes widened.

"No, I'm not kidding. Haven't you recognized something unique about yourself?"

"We're all unique in one way or another," Jesus reminded him.

"You're so modest! But get serious! We're not going to find anybody anywhere even coming close to being like you," he said matter-of-factly.

"Noooo!" Jesus blushed.

"Look! I know what I'm talking about," the old man insisted. Searching the desert floor, his eyes lighted on a heap of stones. "See those stones over there?" he pointed.

"Yeh."

"Do you want to find out just how special you are?"

Special

"Well," Jesus didn't know what to answer.

"Do you or don't you?" the man persisted as he placed his hands on his hips.

"Kinda." Jesus relented.

"It's easy to find out. If you could change those stones into bread—"

"Stones into bread?" Jesus puzzled.

"Yes, you must be famished after a forty-day fast. I know I'd be. And *He* certainly wouldn't begrudge you a simple meal. So kill two birds with one stone. Then you'll have a full stomach and know where you stand with..." he pointed above but avoided looking upward.

"Are you serious?" Jesus was incredulous. "Bread? Don't get me wrong! Right now I'd like to sink my teeth into a hunk of fresh, warm bread. But do you really think that's all his plans are for me?" Tracing letters in the air, Jesus exclaimed, "Jesus The Magician And His Traveling Road Show!" Snapping his fingers he continued, "Abracadabra and *poof!* Wonder Bread!"

Not wanting to appear overbearing, the old man conceded. "OK, OK, It was just a thought I had. Actually, your point about being nothing more than a magician is well taken. You know what's best for yourself."

"Yes, if I'm going to do anything special in life, I'd like to be the one who calls the shots. I don't mean to offend you, but having someone else tell me to do this or that really grates on me," Jesus explained.

"I'm not offended, and I understand exactly what you mean about calling the shots. Besides, if there's anyone who ought to do that, it's you," he said confidentially, placing his hand on Jesus' shoulder.

"You really agree?"

129

"Certainly. But I'm going to tell you something with which you may disagree. I'm convinced you have so much going for you, I'll guarantee you'd be able to do whatever you want, wherever you want, whenever you want! You'd have everybody, and I mean everybody, eating out of the palm of your hand."

Jesus paused to absorb his message. "Hmmmm. I'd have that much power?"

"I told you, you're not just anybody! But you let this modesty thing prevent you from seeing the powerhouse you are," the old man gently scolded. "Think what you could accomplish in life! The people you'd influence! They wouldn't be able to resist you. What does it mean to be special if not to be able to flex your muscles and work your will? People who are special aren't marshmallows or wishy-washy types," he said convincingly.

"How can you guarantee I could do all this?" Jesus wondered.

"By simply repeating slowly after me: 'Nothing or nobody will prevent me from ruling the day,' " he answered.

"That's it?"

"Simple, isn't it? Just repeat it in my presence."

"Why yours?" Jesus sounded dubious.

"Someone has got to hold you accountable for what you say and do!" The old man seemed offended that Jesus should even raise the question. "And when someone uses power as I invite you to use it, invariably that person turns to me for help. All I'm doing is asking you to acknowledge that in advance by way of an oath, a little promise," he added innocently. Not wishing Jesus to consider too carefully what he had

Special

just said, the old man added quickly "So repeat after me: 'Nothing or nobody will prevent me from ruling the day.'"

"It sounds selfish to me."

"It sounds selfish to you," the old man repeated slowly, his mind racing to find a different tack. "And it sounds just a little selfish to me, but you are so much more perceptive and sensitive than I am." The old man recovered beautifully. "Suppose we change it to: 'Whatever I set my mind to do, I can do in a flash like you know who!'" What's nice about these words is no one has to get hurt in order for you to do what you want to do, and—"

"Yes, it sounds better, but I'm not certain it doesn't basically come down to the same thing. What's more, the bit about 'doing in a flash like you know who' is scary. True, it's appealing because when I'm on a high there's nothing I don't think I can do, but I've got second thoughts about swearing to you that I'd attempt living my life like you know who. At times I may think I'm Number One, but in my more sober moments I'm aware I *need* him; I'm *not* him!"

Shaking his head, the old man smiled. "Tsk! Tsk! Tsk! There goes that modesty again. Now I know you're special! And I'll tell you the..." he pointed above and averted his eyes as he had done earlier, "...is lucky to have someone who is so faithful and trusting in his service. What I admire is your willingness to sacrifice your desires to make him happy. You're putting yourself in his hands completely," he gushed.

"I'd like to think I am, yes!" Jesus accepted the compliment.

" 'You'd like to think.' Oh, and the humility! My, oh my, if you aren't something else!" Then very slowly he continued, "And we know you believe he really thinks you're special!"

"I'm not sure I understand what you mean."

"All I mean is you don't know for sure if he wouldn't let you down. Not that you demand proof! You don't, I know. But wouldn't it be nice to be certain? For example, I was just thinking you'd find out if he really thought you were so special by stepping off that temple tower in the distance. If he really cares, he'll see to it that you land on your feet. A simple test, isn't it?"

"Jump off the temple to prove that I'm loved, that I'll never be let down? Or hurt? Yeh, yeh, I've wondered about whether I'm really loved. When I came out of the Jordan I felt so good I thought I was invulnerable and nothing could happen to me. And I've been feeling that way right along, but for one minute the other day, I wasn't sure anymore," Jesus reflected.

"Hmmm, what happened?" Now the old man's curiosity was aroused.

"All I did was stub my toe. Just hit my big toe on a rock. And without thinking I said, 'That's not supposed to happen to me.' "

"You see? That's my point. You want to know for sure you're special, don't you? No second guesses, no doubt, no worm in the apple, etc. So," he stopped and pointed to the Temple, "go there! Let him catch you!"

Jesus didn't move. Instead he looked suspiciously at the old man. Then speaking slowly, he said, "I wouldn't want someone putting himself in a dangerous situation so I'd have to rescue him to prove my love. There are a lot of things I can't do or won't do for others because they have to go through experiences on their own." He paused, looked directly into the old man's eyes, and asked, "Why, then, do I think I ought to be protected by God to prove I'm special?"

"Tell me, then, how do you know you're so special and it isn't just an illusion?" The old man's voice betrayed a thinly disguised tone of sarcasm.

"I think I'm special, but I'm no superstar. And that's going to have to be enough for me. I'm here to trust God, not to test him," Jesus said firmly.

The old man forced a smile. "You have a point. You really do. Well, it's time for me to go. It was so nice talking to you." But never one to give up, he continued as he backed away, "Of course I'll be back. I'd like to continue our little conversation. So for the time being, good-bye." And he disappeared behind the rock where Jesus had first seen him.

Jesus was left alone to reconsider what it meant to be special.

Reflection
What Makes Us Special?

In "Special" Jesus' special experience at the Jordan led him to be tempted. What Abraham Maslow called a peak or mountaintop experience can be a test for anyone to think, "I'm on a different level from the others, a better level. I'm special!" Yet, while Jesus was intrigued by the old man's suggestion that he was better than the others, he didn't yield. What Jesus realized through the tests was that he needed to reflect carefully on the meaning of being special.

We get a lead on what his own understanding of being special might have been if we reconsider how the novices in our introduction came to regard the "special" revelation of the holy in rites of enchantment and disenchantment. We recall that the special revelation of the holy was manifest in the elders masked as the gods. The novices didn't seem to need to look any further for the holy. This was the setup. The letdown was that the holy wasn't specially there and nowhere else. Instead the novices needed to search and find many special persons, places, and things that disclosed the holy. Identifying the holy with the one concrete experience of the gods was intended to be a clue and assist in identifying the holy in other persons, etc. However, as we noted earlier, the temptation is always equating the holy with—rather than through—its signs and symbols, resulting in the sign becoming special in an exclusive sense.

Bearing this in mind, perhaps we can understand being special as the insight that we are revelations of what is wonderful without in fact being The Wonderful. Perhaps Jesus' reflection on the meaning of being special as we describe it here helped him clarify his mission: to proclaim that all are special because all are the wonder-filled revelations of the One who called Jesus "my beloved." The temptation to see himself alone as the beloved is converted into the good news that all are beloved of God—even when they seem to be abandoned as Jesus felt on the cross. And it was other such experiences of abandonment throughout his life (e.g., by the townspeople of Nazareth, Peter, Judas, etc.) that must have led to further disillusionment, which in turn led to further reflection on the different "special" ways in which a person might experience the holy.

What Jesus discovered over and over is that God's beloved is not exempt from suffering. He pointed this out when he told the old man about how he had stubbed his toe and how that had initially disturbed him, especially in light of his baptismal experience of being intensely loved by God. The message must have become clearer as he lived his life: not only is the holy manifest in many persons but it is present in ways which can't be calculated in advance. Protection from suffering, for example, is not the only indication of the presence of the holy, nor is it necessarily an indication of its presence at all. The illusion that being special means one does or doesn't suffer, feels at home or abandoned, experiences God's presence or absence, has to die so the person can be special in God's own way.

Letdowns

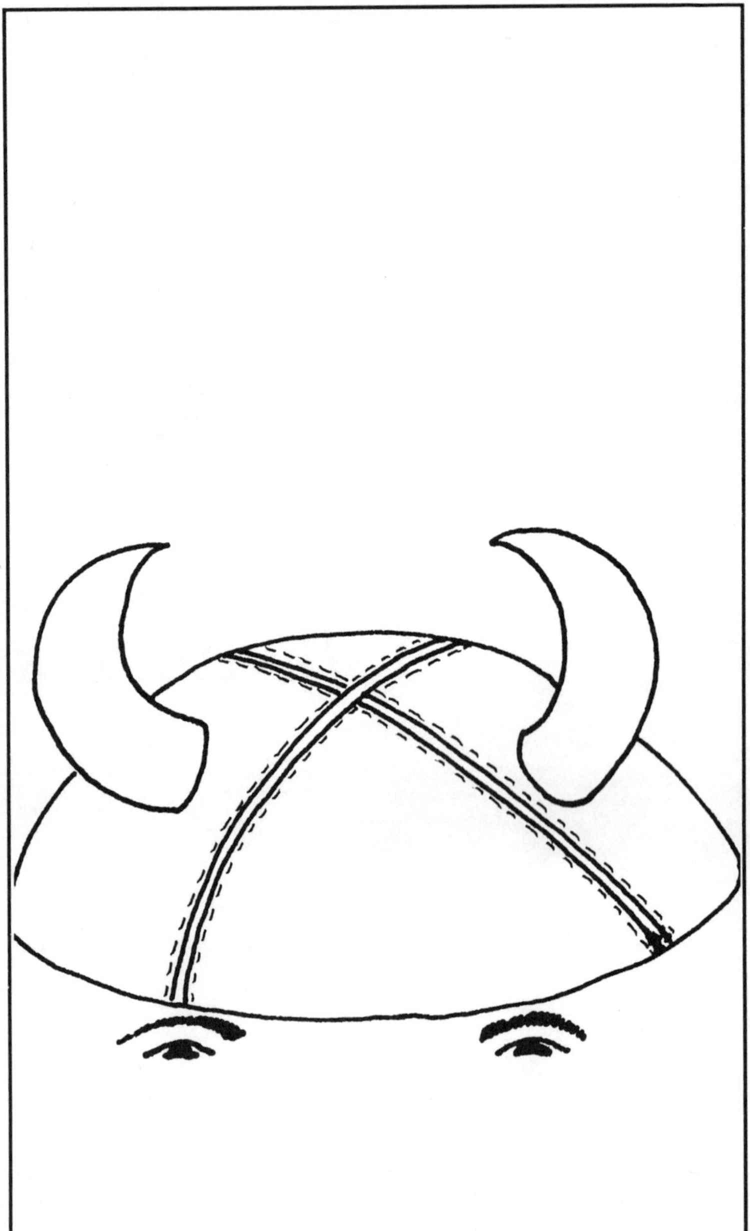

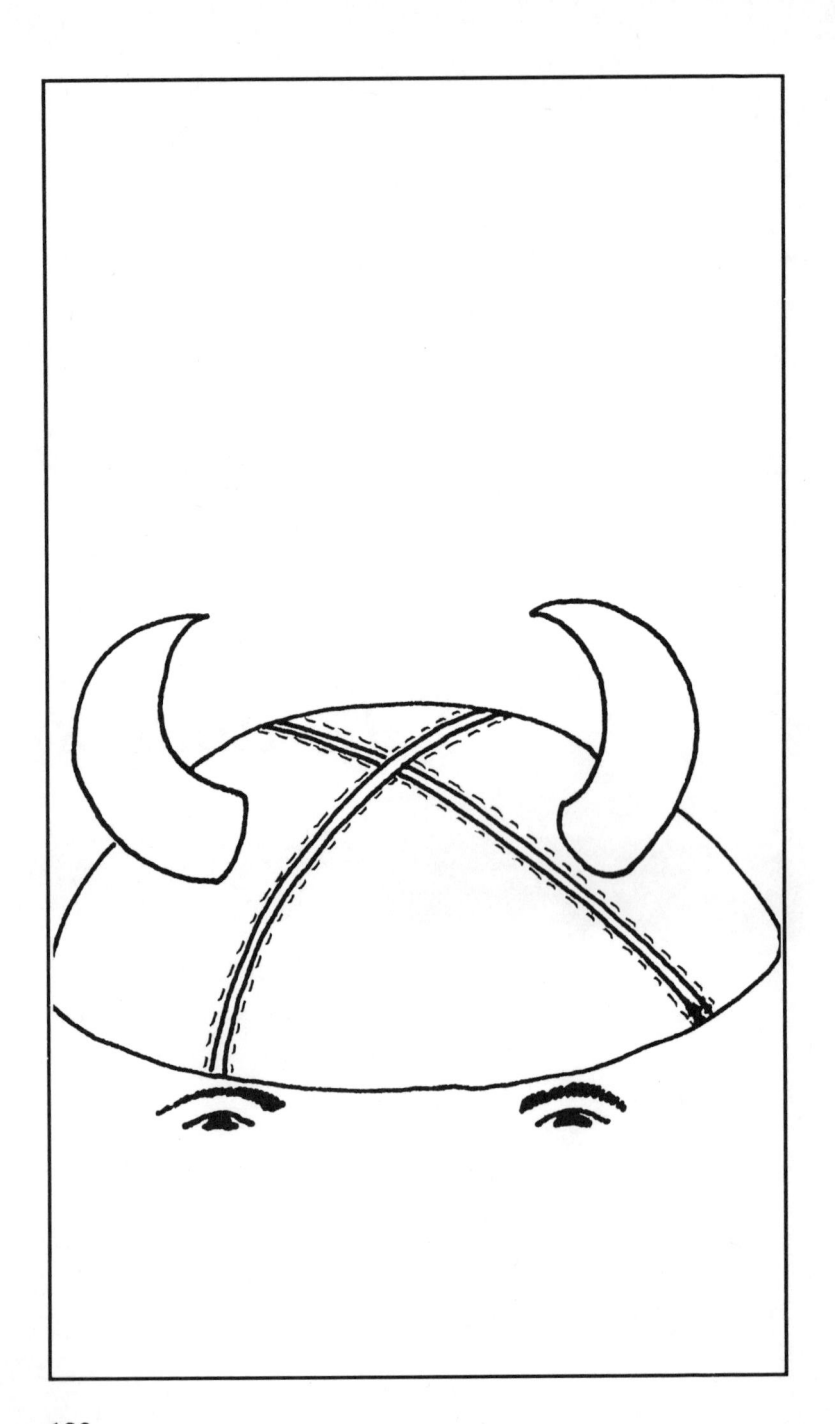

PARANOID

Matthew 12:22-24: A possessed man who was brought to Jesus was blind and mute. He cured the man so that he could speak and see. All in the crowd were astonished. "Might this not be David's son?" they asked. When the Pharisees heard this, they charged, "This man can expel demons only with the help of Beelzebul, the prince of demons."

"Dad, do you know what my teacher told me? I'm gonna be a good writer some day."

"Son, what's her angle? Does she want an invitation to dinner?"

"Grandma, you wouldn't believe what I got from my girlfriend for my birthday: a super-size box of chocolates!"

"Heh! Heh! What's she up to? Probably wants you to take her to the movies next week."

"Ma, would you like to know what Rabbi Stechel told the congregation today? God likes to laugh!"

"Oh, yeh? What's behind his laugh, I wonder?"

Benny had quite a family. Seems they were all able to "see" what devious intentions people really had in mind while appearing to say or do something good. Always certain the worst interpretation was true, they indoctrinated Benny in their point of view.

"I saw Mrs. Rabinowitz giving cookies to the neighbor kids," he reported to his mother. "I'll bet she gave 'em the cookies so they'd mow her lawn," he nodded knowingly.

"You're smart, Benny. You see what's really happening and you tell it like it is," she noted. Benny was delighted. Now he was initiated; he really belonged to the family.

By the time Benny was twenty, he was a master at reading what people really had in mind. Or so he thought!

"You say you want to work for us, Benny?" a prospective employer asked him one day.

"Yeh, sure," Benny nodded.

"May I ask you why you think our firm would want to hire you," he inquired.

"Why? Probably because I'm the cheapest person you can get," Benny answered nonchalantly.

"I hope you do well in your new job, Benny, but it certainly won't be with us!"

And Benny didn't fare any better in successive interviews. "Why do you think we'd want to hire you in our kosher meat market?" the butcher asked.

"To pass off meat nobody else could sell," Benny yawned. And his career as a butcher was over before it started.

"Why should we employ you to sell our clothes?" the proprietor wondered.

"To convince customers the second rate shirts are really top quality as advertised," he answered before being walked to the door.

Paranoid

If Benny didn't fare well in getting a job, he didn't do any better in his personal life either. "What do you mean by that remark?" a friend asked angrily. "Do you think I asked you over for dinner just because I want a favor from you?"

As for girlfriends, one by one in rapid succession they'd come and go because he figured they always had an angle the way they smiled or laughed or held hands with him or gave him a kiss. However forthright they seemed, Benny knew there was always an ulterior motive.

Possessed by some demon, Benny couldn't see clearly, and consequently he was unable to speak intelligibly to others. One day he woke to find the possession complete. Darkness prevailed and his tongue was silenced.

"We don't know what to make of this case," puzzled the physicians as they observed Benny in their clinics. They had no idea why he couldn't see or speak.

"Perhaps he really can see and speak but simply wants attention," one suspicious physician whispered to another.

"I'd say he really wants to show us up, prove we don't know what we're talking about," the other whispered back conspiratorially.

"One thing is clear," a third concluded. "There's more to this than meets the eye. I don't trust him. Let him go!"

So Benny was free to roam the streets—as free as any blind man could be! Relying on his hearing, Benny navigated down streets and alleys, growing more and more frustrated with people misinterpreting everything he did. Bumping into a little boy, Benny was bopped on the head by the boy's irate mother. "Quit bruising little kids," she blasted. "You're trying to scare them, aren't you?"

Old ladies hit him with their canes. "Why are you trailing us so closely? Trying to mug us, I bet?"

"He wants more than that," old men chuckled. "He's just playing dumb, that's all!"

Suspicions hatched wherever Benny paused to catch his breath. He began to wish he had lost his hearing, so painful were the reports he heard about himself and his motives. He was at his wit's end one afternoon and thought seriously of jumping off some building, but he guessed it would be misconstrued as grabbing publicity. Or it would be just his fortune to come crashing down on some poor soul. Then he'd be accused of premeditated murder! As he sat dejected on a corner curb, he felt an arm caress his shoulder.

"Can I help you?" It was a man's voice. Benny shrugged. Why should this man be able to help? Nobody else could. "Give me a chance," the man continued, guessing his thoughts. "It won't hurt." Benny's interest stirred as the man gently hugged him and asked, "Is this a hug or isn't it?" A simple question. Benny nodded yes. Again, the man hugged him so that Benny actually felt good. "Does this feel good?" the man asked. Benny nodded again. A third time the man hugged Benny, and this time he drew Benny's hand up to his own face and eyes.

Benny ran his fingers over the man's mouth, beard, and eyes. He felt tears. Was the man crying? "Yes," Benny concluded. Then the man asked in a voice heavy with emotion, "Would you say I'm playing this from the heart and it's not some game?"

Paranoid

Benny listened, and slowly nodded his head. To have denied the man's sincerity would have been a terrible lie. And as the purity of the stranger's concern hit home, Benny's sight gradually reappeared. At first, he saw the vague outline of the man's body; finally, it was possible to see him clearly: the warm inviting smile, the honest eyes. Behind him were several onlookers fascinated by what they saw. "Maybe this is David's Son?" one asked the others.

But another voice chimed in, "Looks great, doesn't it? But how do you think he's really doing this? It's by the power of the Evil One!" Everybody quieted down. They knew a Pharisee when they heard one and no on cared to tangle with him. But the silence was short lived. One who knew firsthand what it was like to suspect bad for good cried, "No! No!" Benny looked directly into Jesus' eyes. "What he's done is from the heart. Really! There's no reason to read anything evil into it at all. If I've learned any lesson, it's that one!" Benny was no longer mute. He spoke the truth as he saw it.

Jesus thanked Benny and then turned to his detractor. However, Benny was so elated over what had happened he could not follow what was being said. All he knew is that there were many others on the same road as he had already traveled. His heart ached for others. But one thing was certain. He had been there and he didn't intend to go there again.

Reflection

*Deep down I'm nobody
because everybody let me down.*

When we fear we can trust nobody, we are acknowledging how hurt and insecure we really are. Benny in "Paranoid" illustrates the destructive character of paranoia.

Benny's paranoia comes back to haunt him later in the story as he perceives others' mistrust of him. It is a terrifying experience that leaves him feeling like nobody because he thinks everybody is against him. While we may think Benny's paranoia is unusual, actually we don't need to look very far for other more common examples. Technically this kind of mistrust can be called xenophobia: a fear or hatred of strangers—whoever isn't us.

Consider Iran's attitude toward the world; or a fundamentalist's designation of society as secular, humanist, and godless; or the Church's centuries of mistrust toward women (out to work their wiles on men, naturally). Then there's the stereotypical suspicion of a black man running down the street ("What's he running from?") and the Jews ("What are they up to—again?") We do have our own setups, illusions, assumptions, and biases that embody a conviction that a person or a group can't be trusted no matter what they say or do that indicates otherwise.

Benny's letdown comes from getting a good dose of his own medicine, and it is only when he is rendered completely helpless that he is capable of being helped by Jesus. He has to experience complete abandonment before any transformation can take place.

What do our suspicions of others tell us about ourselves and our own insecurities? If we are uneasy with most of the people we meet, then do we really trust ourselves and our relational abilities? Is it true that basically we feel like nobody because we think everybody is against us?

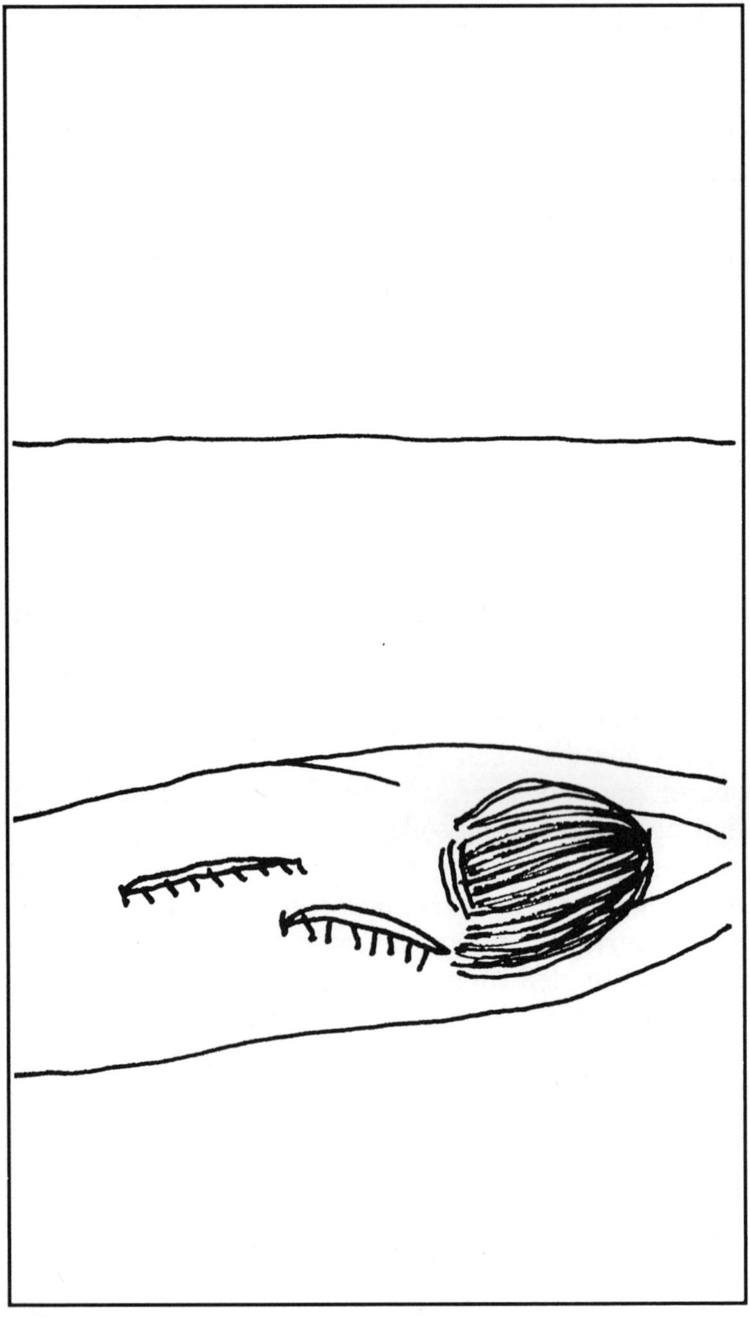

SAM: A HERO IN SPITE OF HIMSELF

Luke 10:30: "There was a man going down from Jerusalem to Jericho who fell prey to robbers. They stripped him, beat him, and then went off leaving him half-dead."

The man had been lying three hours in a ditch somewhere between Jerusalem and Jericho. Badly beaten and blood trickling from scalp wounds, he lay motionless, moaning softly.

Alternately skipping and gliding, a priest made his way down that road. He appeared to be rehearsing for some liturgical event as he self-consciously folded his hands, extended them, and folded them again all the while chanting "Sanctus! Sanctus! Sanctus! Haec diem fecit Dominus! (This is the day which the Lord has made)." At one point he halted, took out a small hand mirror, moistened his right finger, smoothed his right eyebrow, then moistened his left finger and smoothed the other eyebrow. Examining as much of his jowled face as possible, he sighed "Gorgeous!"

LETDOWNS

No sooner had the word passed his lips than he spied the injured man. "What's this? What's this?" he muttered. Quickly sizing up the situation, he nodded knowingly and dismissed what he saw with a wave of his hand. "He's pretending, pretending," the priest chanted. "Putting on a show! But it's a trap. Once I stop to help and *bang*, I'm on the ground, my wallet gone! I've seen it all before, before. We do it all the time. I should know." Circling the wounded man, he continued, "Hauling out our costumes, we rehearse our actions. Then, what a show, what a show! Prancing here, dancing there, swinging censors and singing halleluias, looking awed and awesome, but," he winked at the man who stirred slightly, "faking it, really faking it, simply faking it. We're really after the money, too! So, you see, I've seen it all before. I know. You're pretending! A real gas! A hit! But just a show, don't I know?"

Having circled the man several times, skipping and gliding, hands folded, then extended, eyebrows moistened, and latin chanted, he grinned, sang "toodle-oo," blew the man a kiss, and skipped merrily away.

An hour passed and no one came. Still another hour elapsed. Finally, in the distance, a Levite, a great scholar, came along. Preoccupied with his lofty thoughts, he almost didn't see the injured man. However, the soft moaning was just loud enough to attract the Levite's attention. Startled, he gazed into the ditch. "What's this? What's this?" he exclaimed in horror. Lifting his arms high in the air, he turned around several times as though addressing an audience, "Someone's bloodied, someone's bruised. Tsk! Tsk! Tsk! Horrible! Horrible! It's a pity, it's a pity! No one's safe anymore. Here's an innocent! A victim! What to do? Who's to care for him? I see no one around. No one. What's this world coming to? Where are the police? The medics? His neighbors? Friends? Wife? Children? Pets? Is there no one, no one who'll help? By God, where's God? Ah yes! We're all alone. You and me, brother, we're all alone. No one can be counted on. I suffer with you in this existential void!" Lowering his arms, he glanced at his watch, "Hmmmm, time to go." And without so much as a parting glance, he dashed off down the road.

No more than five minutes had elapsed before another figure emerged on the horizon—actually, two figures. A thin, frail- looking, frizzy-red-headed chap by the name of Sam stumbled down the road, coaxing his reluctant mule. "C'mon Moose; it's OK. You don't need to worry," Sam urged as he anxiously scanned the road and bushes for any signs of danger. Apparently unconvinced, Moose needed to be tugged, cajoled, and threatened every couple of yards. Sam was so desperate to clear that notorious stretch of road that he was about ready to abandon Moose to an uncertain fate when his eyes fell on the wounded man.

"Oh no!" he panicked, his pale complexion blanching even more. Grabbing his oversized sunglasses from somewhere deep inside his tunic, he plopped them on, averted his eyes, and muttered, "I didn't see him! I didn't see him!" Desperately yanking Moose's halter, he wiped the beads of perspiration from his brow and tried to convince himself: "My mind is playing terrible tricks on me. It must be the heat." Moose didn't agree. The mule brayed and nudged Sam repeatedly in the direction of the injured man. "OK, OK, don't get pushy," Sam complained as he realized he couldn't deny what was so obvious to Moose.

149

"I'll go and take a peek, but that's all." Edging cautiously toward the body, Sam covered his eyes, fearful of what he might see. When he got close enough, he peeked between his fingers and, seeing the man's bloodied head, gasped "Ohhh, all that blood! I'm getting sick." Sam made a beeline for a clump of bushes where he disappeared temporarily.

When he finally staggered out, he shook an accusing finger at Moose. "It's all your fault!" Sam reached the saddlebags and removed a flask of wine and took a swig. So agitated was he that when he finally knelt to offer the injured man a drink, the wine spilled all over the man's head. Attempting to make the best of it, he sighed, "Maybe it'll help those ugly cuts on your forehead, Bucko." Sam gingerly touched the open wounds and winced. "Oh, I've got to do something about these cuts. But I haven't got anything to stop the bleeding except for this." He reached into his tunic and retrieved a colorful scarf. "My new monogrammed bandanna. I paid thirty shekels for this!" He paused. "My bandanna?" Sam got up decisively and started walking toward the mule. "My bandanna," he said almost with a note of defiance.

Moose didn't agree. The mule brayed several times, turned and stood so its behind stared Sam in the face. "Sure, easy for you to be so righteous. It's not your bandanna," he mumbled resentfully. "OK, OK, I'll go back."

Returning to the man, he took the bandanna, stroked the gold-embroidered monogram, and said, "I hope you know what this means to me, Bucko. This is your thirty-shekel Band-Aid!" Wrapping it carefully around the man's head, he said, "Bucko, it's time to get you to your feet, if that's possible. Can you get up?"

Sam: A Hero in Spite of Himself

The man managed to speak a few words. "Oy vay Gevalt! Ich hab nich kan koich. Ich bin krank. (Oh God, help, I have no strength. I am not well.)"

Sam's eyes widened. "Oh my God! You aren't even one of us. I should have known. Those curls around your ears are a dead giveaway! You're different!" The injured man looked directly into Sam's eyes, a frightened look on his face. Sam's own eyes moistened as he commented, "Yeh! You're different all right, but I'm sure you're as scared to be here as I am, and that's where we're the same." Bending down, Sam placed the man's arm around his shoulder and attempted to get him to his feet. Realizing how difficult this would be, he motioned to the mule. "Hey Moose! Over here!" To Sam's surprise the mule promptly obeyed, for the first time in years. "Sure, anything for a stranger! But for me? No way!" Sam grunted. Hoisting the man to his feet, Sam managed to drape him over Moose's back— only because Moose had knelt down on two of its legs to receive the man.

Having secured the man on Moose's back, Sam said, "OK, Moose, let's go. We still have to get to an inn and drop off Bucko. Remind me to leave a note with the innkeeper. I want my bandanna back when I pass through town again." Moose brayed and the three of them, Moose, Sam, and Bucko journeyed off into the sunset.

Which of the three proved a neighbor to the man who fell in with the robbers?

Reflection

*Deep down I'm nobody
because it's a dog-eat-dog world.*

Unfortunately, the priest in "Sam" never became aware of how paranoid he was and therefore could not be helped. The priest's bias helps us understand how projection can work either in favor or against the person projecting. Sam was able to be compassionate to the extent that he saw his own fear in the stranger's face, whereas the priest projected his own capacity for deception into the stranger. As a result the priest felt no obligation to help the stranger. He interpreted the world as a stage on which people are performing—putting on good shows perhaps, but just performing. He was held in bondage by a disillusionment that led him to cast a suspicious eye on every person whom he met.

The Levite was as cynical as the priest. Mouthing words of concern, he was no more prepared to help the wounded man than was the priest. Projecting his own indifference into all the people whom he named, he then glanced at his watch and left the wounded man as he found him.

Do we view others as only interested in their wellbeing? Do we categorically dismiss all politicians as corrupt? All religious people as hypocritical? All welfare recipients as lazy? Do we really think we can't trust anybody, at all? A universal condemnation is another way of saying deep down we're nobody because it's a dog-eat-dog world.

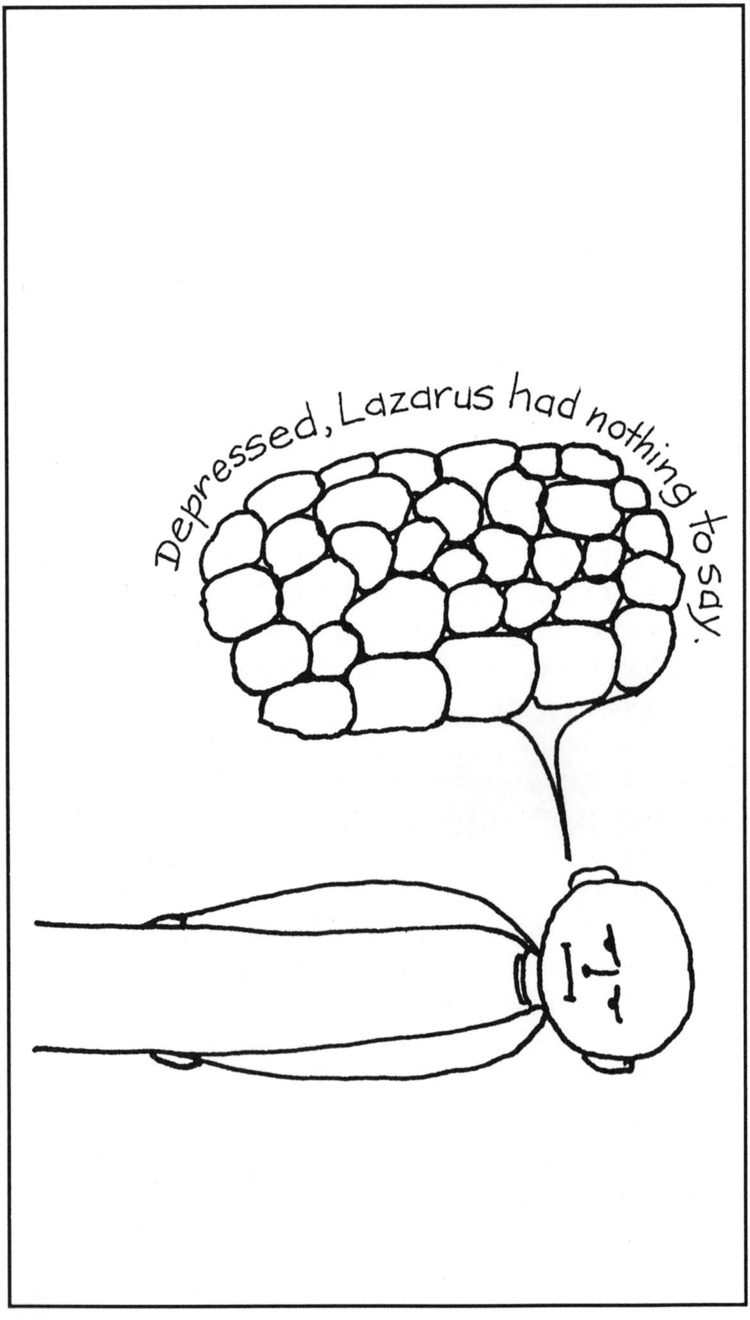
Depressed, Lazarus had nothing to say.

LAZARUS

John 11:1ff: There was a certain man named Lazarus who was sick.

He wanted to die before his time. Lazarus had decided if he couldn't be the man he was, he wasn't a man and he might as well be dead.

He had taken satisfaction in knowing no one his age came close to being as agile as he was. Not only had he taken delight in knowing this, he had reveled in knowing everybody else knew it. He used wave to admirers as he walked a fast-paced six miles every day. Hoofing it down the street, he had been more aware of the neighbors applauding him in his seventy-eighth year than he had been of his labored breathing. And could he dance! He'd go to the local dance hall with his sisters and dance up a storm on Saturday evenings. He had loved to kick up his heels and glide across the dance floor in ways no one ten years his younger could do. A glow would come over his face whenever a woman younger than himself asked to dance with him. And off he'd go, doing the rumba or fox trot or polka,

LETDOWNS

even if he was winded or tired. After all, he had thought, if younger men tired of dancing sooner than he, why shouldn't he expect fatigue?

Yes, Lazarus had more energy at 78 than many a man at age 50. He was the only man in the neighborhood who prayed it would snow so he'd be able to shovel and strut his strength. No matter if he exhausted himself more quickly than in the past. All he needed to keep him going was the "My, my, you're really unbelievable" observation of an awestruck neighbor.

So how did Lazarus reach the point of wanting to die before his time? Because in spite of the exhilaration and admiration he experienced at age 78, it was becoming painfully apparent that he didn't want to admit at age 78 he wasn't 48.

"I'm a little weak in the knees. But a few vitamins will do it," he told Martha one day.

"Yes, a few vitamins will do it," Martha agreed.

But a few vitamins didn't do it.

"It's the onions in the salad, Martha. They make my knees wobble."

"Of course, of course, Lazarus. No more onions."

But it wasn't the onions.

"Martha, Martha, it's the yolk in the egg. It zaps the strength from my hands."

"Most likely, most likely, Lazarus. No more yolks."

And it wasn't the yolks.

"Not enough bananas, Martha. Cramps in the legs."

"More bananas, many more bananas," Martha conceded.

But the knees continued to wobble, although not excessively so. And the hands weren't all that much stronger, but not unduly weak. And the legs were not young Astaire's but certainly not those of a cripple. Yet, for Lazarus it all spelled disaster. He was done for and done in. He might as well be dead. So, depressed he took to his bed. "I'd like to die now," he'd say to Martha or to Mary or to whomever came into his room. "What's there to live for? I'm not the man I was. And I never will be."

"He wants to die. He wants to die before his time. He says he's not the man he was and he never will be," his sisters and friends repeated to one another when they'd leave his room. Shaking their heads they always added, "Why can't he just be the man he is?"

As the days rolled by and the nights grew longer, Lazarus withdrew more and more from the land of the living. "Leave me alone. Leave me alone," he said to anyone who came to visit. Day in and day out he stared at the drapes drawn over all the windows as he lay wrapped in a thin white sheet. Refusing to bathe or shave himself, Lazarus soon got his wish to be alone. Fewer and fewer people came to visit him. Even Mary and Martha found it difficult to enter his room as the stench grew worse and worse. He had hoped to die, and for all practical purposes he had done just that. His sisters had hoped he would not die before his time but now they despaired—despaired and wondered why their friend Jesus had not come sooner than he did to look in on Lazarus. They had sent for him, but it seemed forever before he finally arrived. "Too late! Too late!" they said as he entered their home. "He's died before his time!"

"Died? Lazarus has died? Not so. Not so." Jesus said as he looked in the direction of the room where Lazarus lay. "Let me in his room. No man should die before his time. It cannot be." Jesus didn't remove his gaze from the closed door to Lazarus' room as he spoke to Martha and Mary.

"But the smell is so great. The smell in the room is the smell of a dead man. It will be too much for you," Martha protested.

He ignored the protest and repeated, "No man should die before his time. He must live his life until he dies and only then has he a right to die."

"But what can you do or say that will bring him back?" Mary asked.

"Leave that to me," Jesus answered quietly. Then he moved toward the door, swung it open, and cried out, "Lazarus, Lazarus. It's not time to die. You can't die before your time. So your knees still wobble, your hands aren't Goliath's, and your legs aren't Astaire's. There's still life there and you better not die before your time. No, you aren't going to die before your time. Get up, Lazarus, get up! You aren't going to die before your time. Where do you get off thinking and feeling you have a right to give up before your time? Stop dwelling in the land of the living dead. There's little enough time for us to live and love." Tears forming in his eyes, Jesus added almost inaudibly, "No one knows that more than me." Then, his voice cracking with emotion, Jesus wailed, "Get up Lazarus, get up!"

A stony silence greeted Jesus' words. But then from within the room sobbing sounds broke the silence. After a minute or so the sobbing subsided and the creak, creak, creak of bed springs followed. Finally, a gaunt-looking Lazarus, wrapped in his white sheet, appeared at the door. At first he said nothing, but then, looking intently into Jesus' eyes, he picked up on Jesus' words and said "The time is short to live and love. It's not right to die before our time?"

"Never, never," Jesus added quickly.

Lazarus examined the sheet in which he had wrapped himself for so long and he whispered "It's not right for me to die before my time. It's not right." He stopped, moved backward a few steps as if he were going to go back into his room but instead moved forward. Pirouetting, he dropped the sheet and cried out, "It ain't right to die before my time! My knees wobble, my hands aren't Goliath's, and I don't have Astaire's legs, but it ain't right to die before my time."

"No," Jesus said as he looked out the window at the stormclouds gathering over Jerusalem. "My legs wobble and I have fears of my own, but," and here he smiled at Lazarus, "it ain't right to die before my time either, and no one will stop me from living before that time." Putting his arms around Martha and Mary, he sounded a note of joy. "Let's celebrate! Lazarus is back from the dead."

Reflection

Deep down I'm nobody because my body let me down.

Central to Lazarus' identity was his belief that strength and agility were essential to being a man. Emphasis on the youthful body as constituting masculinity or femininity is what many advertisers would have us believe, particularly people in the cosmetic and plastic surgery business. It is understandable, then, as we age and experience losses in hearing, seeing, remembering, etc., that our self-esteem can diminish. Set up to believe being an ideal man or woman is being youthful, during a period of disillusionment we have to redefine what it means to be a man or woman.

This reevaluation frequently takes place during a midlife transition. Carl Jung, the Swiss psychiatrist, maintained that midlife is the time to move toward developing a deeper interior life. It is conceivable that a depression at this time is an indication that energies ordinarily available for extroverted activities are now withdrawn and turned inward to stimulate unconscious processes so that new possibilities for growth become available. If this is the case, then depression symbolizes not only death but new life waiting to be born.

Christ's injunction to Lazarus not to die before his time is an invitation to experience life in ever-new ways. How do we view the times in our own lives when we seem to have reached a dead end? Do we regard some of the darker moments as simply occasions for despair or is it possible that, as was the case with Lazarus, it isn't time to die because something is yet to be born?

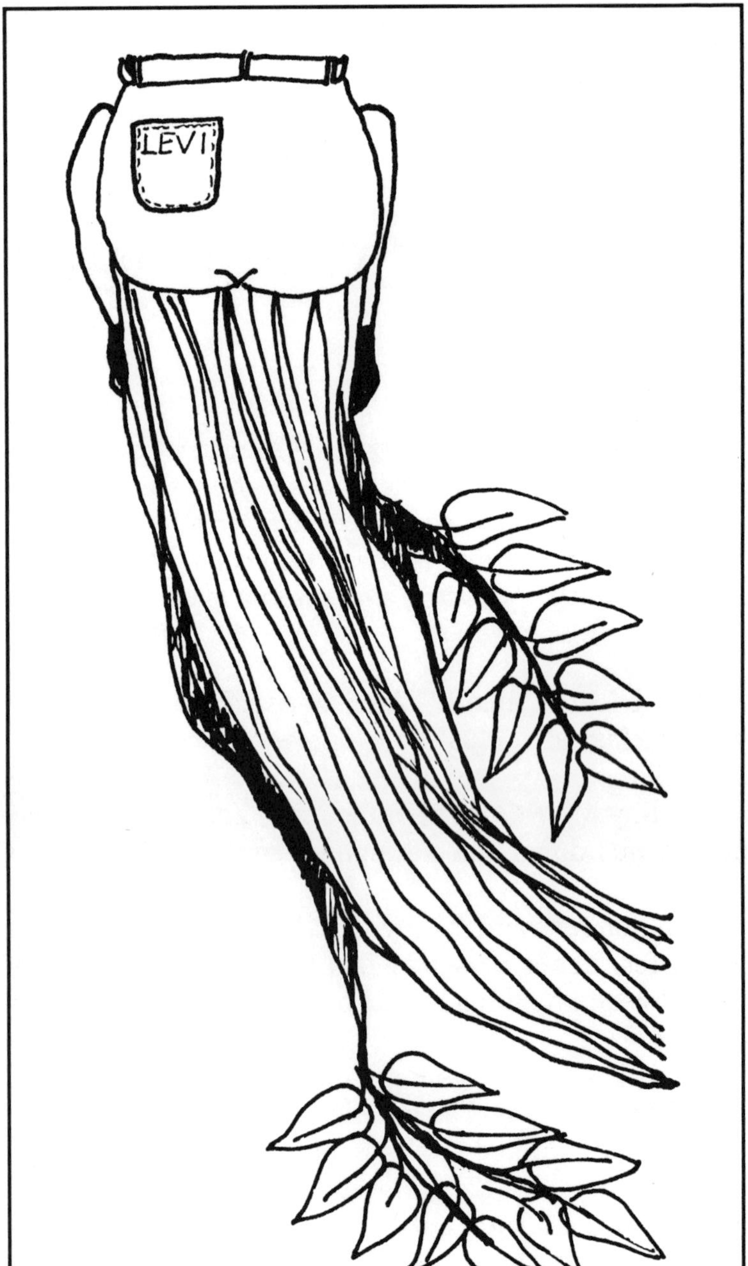
LEVI

LITTLE MAN

Luke 19:1-3: Entering Jericho, Jesus passed through the city. There was a man there named Zacchaeus, the chief tax collector and a wealthy man. He was trying to see what Jesus was like, but being small of stature, was unable to do so because of the crowd.

"Oh, I feel so small," Zacchaeus said one morning at breakfast as he looked at his wife, Leah. "So very small!"

"Well, you are only five feet tall, Zack," Leah said as she put down the newspaper and studied Zack's figure.

"I'm not referring to my size. I'm talking about the way I feel about myself. I feel this high." Zacchaeus bent low and held his hand about five inches from the ground.

"That is small," Leah agreed. "So what is the matter? Why do you feel so small?"

Zacchaeus walked to the window of their luxurious apartment in the King David, which overlooked the city. "I'm not sure, Leah. I've been thinking about it for some time. Working for the Romans doesn't help. I know I wanted the job, but taxing my countrymen is sinking pretty low."

"Why didn't you think about that when you applied for the job?" Leah asked.

"Because I wanted to make money and have the kind of things that would make me feel important: this hotel room, nice clothes, good food. I wanted to feel big, something I never felt before. No one ever noticed me and I wanted them to see that I had made it. I wanted them to say, 'See, that is a big man coming down the street.'"

"And it hasn't worked out that way, has it?" Leah seemed to understand what he was feeling.

Zacchaeus was silent for a moment. "No, it hasn't. I hear them talking as I go down the street. 'There's the big shot. Ripping off all the poor folk again.' They don't like me out there. I tell you, they hate my guts. Just the other day when I was collecting money in one of their homes, someone let the air out of my tires. And that isn't the first time that has happened. I feel just like the tires look—deflated! What am I going to do?"

Leah started gathering the breakfast dishes. "I'm not sure, Zack. I'd like to talk a little bit more with you about it, but I have an early appointment at the hairdressers. Later we can talk."

"Yes," Zacchaeus said. "I have to get going too. I have to get into downtown Jericho to my office. Someone is coming to see me."

Wondering just what he was going to do, Zacchaeus left the house. He was more desperate than he had let on. He didn't want Leah upset, but he really felt very low, very low indeed. He got into his car and drove the three miles into the downtown area. There was an

Little Man

unusual amount of traffic that morning, and he couldn't understand why so many people had gathered in the park across the street from his office building.

When he got out of his car, he heard people talking about Jesus. Jesus was speaking in the park. Jesus? Zacchaeus had heard about Jesus. He had even considered trying to see him privately but had given up on the idea. What could Jesus do for him? Now, however, he wanted to hear what Jesus had to say. He wanted to hear anything he had to say.

Zacchaeus walked across the street into the park. There was such a crowd that, because he was so short, Zacchaeus couldn't see Jesus at all. He wondered if he could push his way closer, but he couldn't because he simply didn't have the weight to do it. He looked around and his eyes landed on a tree close by. He would climb that tree, that's what he would do. Then he looked at what he was wearing—his flashy pin-striped suit—and he laughed! It wasn't exactly the kind of clothes a person would wear to climb a tree. At a time like this, he thought, what difference did it make? "I'm tired of trying to look smart when I feel so low."

So Zacchaeus took a deep breath, made his way to the tree, and began to climb up the tree. It wasn't easy since he hadn't climbed a tree for years. Once he was up the tree, he chuckled to himself. "I'm up a tree all right and I have been for some time, longer than I've been up this one. I might as well go out on a limb as well." He climbed out on a sturdy limb, held on tight, and looked down. There was Jesus, right in the middle of the crowd. Zacchaeus looked and listened intently as he tried to pick up whatever Jesus was saying.

Zacchaeus had only been up there a minute when Jesus happened to look up and see Zacchaeus.

165

LETDOWNS

Zacchaeus' eyes met Jesus's, and Jesus let out a big laugh. Such a laugh! Had it been anyone else who laughed, Zacchaeus would have felt twice as small as he did. When Jesus laughed, however, Zacchaeus wanted to laugh as well. It surely had to be a funny sight, Zacchaeus thought. Now Jesus was asking the person next to him who it was that he was looking at in the tree. He was also getting more information than he had sought. Zacchaeus began to feel terrible. He felt that Jesus was getting a bad picture of him and would soon be scolding him.

Zacchaeus seemed to wait forever. But Jesus did not stop smiling. No, he put his hands to his mouth and shouted above the din of the crowd, "Zacchaeus, I want to come to your place for dinner. We've got a lot to talk about! C'mon down from there!" Zacchaeus' eyes opened wide. Jesus wanted to come to his place for dinner! Zacchaeus was ecstatic. Jesus hadn't put him down or called him a sinner or a no good so-and-so as other preachers might have done. No, he wanted to come and have dinner at Zacchaeus' place. Zacchaeus scrambled down the tree as fast as he could. He had gone out on a limb and landed safely in Jesus' presence.

The crowd grumbled, of course. They didn't like the idea at all that Jesus was going to have dinner with the big shot. Zacchaeus had made up his mind then and there that he was going to give up half of his belongings to the poor as a way of making up for the way he had treated people. He also decided to pay those he had cheated four times as much as he had cheated them.

Jesus looked at Zacchaeus and told him, "Salvation has come to your house today." What that meant is

Little Man

that what Zacchaeus' money, clothes, expensive suite of rooms, and imported cigars couldn't do, Jesus did. And what was that? Jesus made him feel ten feet tall! Salvation had indeed come to Zacchaeus.

NEEDS

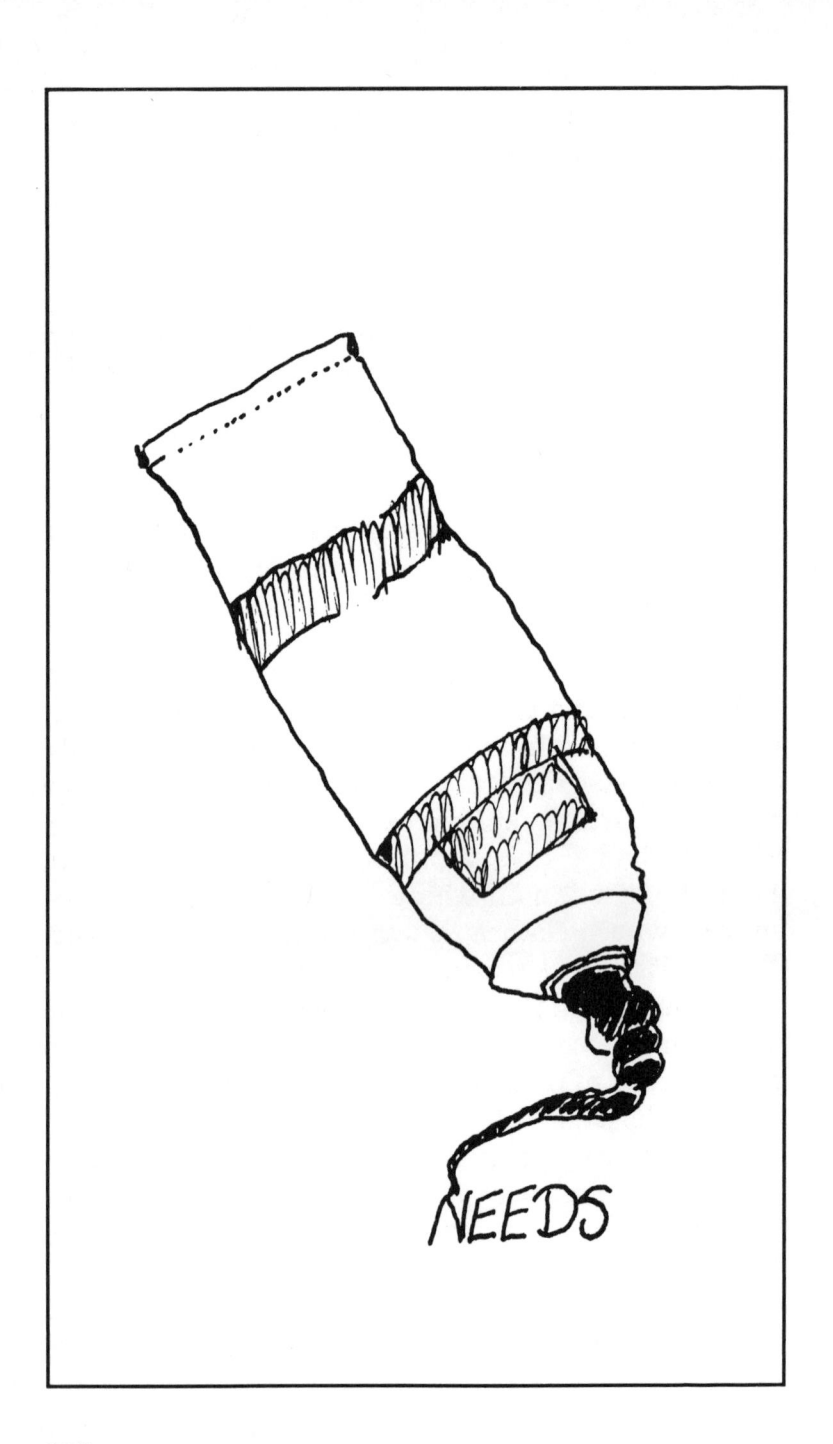

BETTER OFF

Luke 18:9: Jesus then spoke this parable addressed to those who believed in their own self-righteousness while holding everyone else in contempt.

The two men hadn't seen one another for years. It had been so long that at first they didn't even recognize one another in the back of the temple. Nor would they have recognized one another had it not been for Sam. As he was about to make his way up to the front where he had always sat, his eyes fell on the last pew. There he saw a man whose face was gaunt and unshaven, whose clothes appeared rumpled and soiled. That in itself was not unusual. Lots of men like that sat in the back of the temple. But something about the man's profile caught Sam's attention. Then, with a growing look of recognition, Sam said, "Fred? Are you Fred Fredericks?"

The man started as he looked at Sam and replied hesitantly, "Yes, why yes, I'm Fred." Then his look too registered recognition. "Sam...you're Sam Trevor?"

"Yes, I sure am," Sam said with an assurance that contrasted markedly with Fred's hesitancy. "Fred, it's been years. How have you been doing?" he asked, though he guessed that Fred couldn't be too well off if his present appearance were any indication. Without waiting for an answer, Sam plowed on, "Are you still in the insurance business? You were really going great guns about ten years ago, weren't you? As I recall, you had pretty much built the business on your own, hadn't you?" Sam nodded his approval as he added, "I admire people who can go it alone. We'd be better off with more people like us who don't need to rely on handouts from the government or anyone else—"

"I, I lost the business," Fred interrupted. "I really don't have a business anymore."

"Oh, sorry to hear that. You have to know what you're doing if you want to be a success. I'm happy to say my feed business is pretty well off. I guess I've just got a good head for business." Sam laughed with the confidence that comes from knowing who you are and what you are about in life.

"How are Mary and the kids?" Sam changed the subject since he wasn't particularly interested in understanding self-made failures, just self-made successes.

"Mary? Well, Mary and I split up six months ago."

"Split up?" Sam had a slightly judgmental tone in his voice. "I guess that can happen if the old lines of communication aren't open. I'm happy to say Marge and I have got our channels open all the time. But I'd have to admit, I'm probably more responsible than she is for keeping our marriage so well off. You've got to work at it. I keep telling Marge that. She doesn't always see it my way at first, but sooner or later I get her to come around.

"So, you say you're separated. Must be hard on the kids? Who are they with? You or Mary?"

"They're with Mary. She has custody," Fred said sadly.

"Not too much on top of things there either, hey Fred?" Sam chided, though he figured the kids were probably better off with Mary.

Fred cleared his throat. "I guess not, Sam. It's all been downhill for me since I started drinking five years ago. In fact, I'm at the point where I'd just like to take a gun and end it all! Haven't you ever felt that way?" Fred looked to Sam for some sign of comprehension.

"No," Sam answered without any hesitation. "I've always been able to handle things. I like challenges and I've never had to rely on booze or drugs when things got tough. And as for suicide, I thank God I've got a strong mind. I never think of those things. If you live a good, clean life, then you don't need all those crutches just to get through. What do your kids think of all this?" Sam asked with some disgust.

"My kids? Well, they're having their own problems. I try to help them, but I don't think I'm doing such a great job," Fred confessed.

"Just let them know who's boss. My kids look up to me. Every now and then they get out of line, but they know what I expect of them. They never get smart with me. Why, I've even talked to them about their future and they agree that they're better off following the old man's advice than trying their own cockamamie schemes." Sam winked at Fred and added, "The trick is being a good role model."

"Well, I can't claim I've been that," Fred admitted. "I love them, but I certainly couldn't prove that by some of the things I've said and done. You know Sam, I used to think I was everything you are, but the truth is I'm really unglued. I really need help."

"Hey, don't talk that way!" Sam shot back as if Fred had admitted to having leprosy. "Pull yourself together. Just put your mind to it. You're better off without anybody's help. You start thinking that way and you'll get nobody's respect. You want your wife back and your kids to look up to you? Are you the man in the family or not? When I come to the temple, like today, I thank God that I'm a guy who knows who he is, what he wants, and how to go about getting it. Do you think that God would have it any other way?" Sam ended with a flourish.

Fred studied Sam for a minute and then responded. "It's strange, Sam. I don't seem to know who I am anymore, what I want, or how to go about getting it. And that's exactly why I came here today. I don't even know how to pray for what I need." His voice quavered. "All I know is that I need, I need badly. Need is my only name now, my only name. Do you understand that, Sam?"

Sam stood nonplussed for a moment but quickly regained the self-assurance that had brought him to the temple and would shortly conduct him to his front row seat. "I'm afraid I don't, Fred. It was nice talking to you, but now I have to go and pray. The Lord is waiting to hear from me." And with that Sam strode to the front of the temple while Fred remained huddled in the back.

Who do you think was better off?

Reflection

Deep down I'm nobody because I let myself down.

In our reflection on the different reactions we experience after betrayal, we noted that self-rejection is particularly painful. If we have been under the impression we were successful in our career or marriage or other endeavors and then experience setbacks in any areas of life, we might conclude not only that we have been let down but also that we have let ourselves down. Along with the sense of failure is the experience of depression.

In both "Little Man" and "Better Off," we read of men with low self-esteem, guilt, remorse, and loss of direction. Fred Fredericks did more poorly than Zacchaeus because he had experienced losses on all fronts, whereas Zacchaeus' marriage was still intact. However, both men experienced the blues, and it was in that experience—not in spite of it—that they began to see themselves, stripped of the illusions that had previously propped up inauthentic lives.

At the point of disillusionment, self-hatred became a very real option. They had reached an impasse, the kind of impasse we recall from our introduction. They were in the dark and didn't know which way to turn. Yet, contrary to appearances, it is in the dark that relationships can achieve new depths as motives and desires are purified. For both Fred Fredericks and Zacchaeus, this purification meant they couldn't justify or prove themselves acceptable. Acceptability was out of their hands and in the hands of the only one who could justify them, namely, God. Without denying the real danger that self-rejection may lead to despair, we can affirm the creative possibilities in these "negative" experiences.

Have we ever been brought to the point of despair and discovered, rather, a new point of departure? In the midst of our disillusionments, have we ever come to new insights about our relationships, insights that have deepened, not destroyed those relationships? Finally, have such experiences helped us to realize that even though we have let ourselves down, we don't really need to conclude we are nobody?

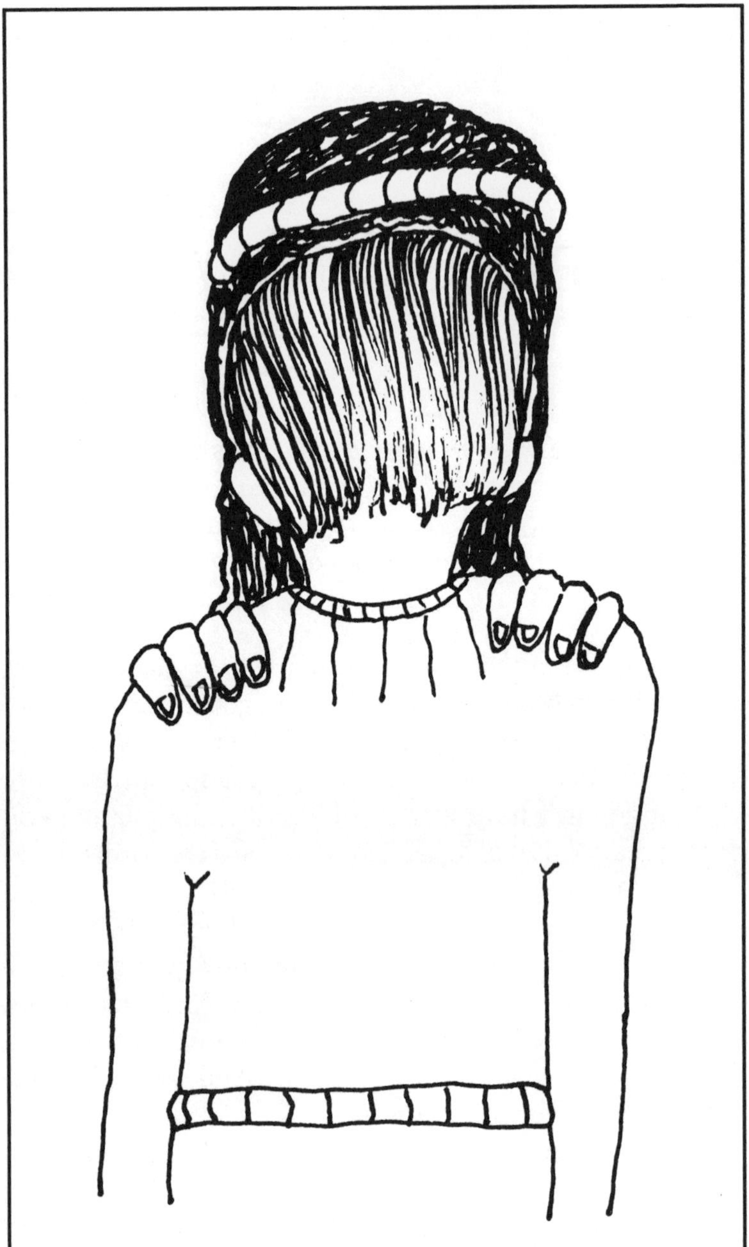

BECOMING A MAN

Luke 7:11-12: Soon afterward Jesus went to a town called Naim, and his disciples and a large crowd accompanied him. As he approached the gate of the town a dead man was being carried out, the only son of a widowed mother.

Crying wasn't considered manly, at least not in Ezra's household. "Josh, we've just got to learn to take it on the chin," Ezra lectured his son, who had been bloodied in a brawl one day on the school playground. "Crying won't help you at all. All it'll do is make you look weak." Ezra dried the telltale tearstains from Joshua's face, looked at him directly, smiled, and urged him, "Make your dad proud of you. OK?"

"OK," Joshua agreed as he quickly wiped away the few last tears that had just appeared. And he was off. He learned never to cry when he got into fights, even if his friends cheated and he lost. And when he saw any of the other kids hurting?

"Josh, I know your friend Benny is upset because his parakeet died, but that's no reason for you to cry. Crying won't bring the parakeet back, will it? Make your dad proud of you. No tears now, huh?"

"OK," Joshua agreed. He got the message as he had earlier. No crying and Dad would be proud of him.

And when Joshua's favorite grandpa died, he proved himself a real man. No tears for grandpa. Just a stiff upper lip. Boy! Was dad ever proud of Joshua then! The two of them stood there at the gravesite, side by side, shoulder to shoulder, as Grandpa's body was lowered into the ground. Neither of them shed a tear. Ezra's wife, Suzanna, cried, but Ezra expected that. "She breaks down easily, your mother." Ezra was almost apologetic. Winking at Joshua, he whispered, "We can forgive her, can't we?"

"Oh yeh," Joshua winked back.

"But you, you're a man. You're strong like your dad. Right?"

"Right, Dad," Joshua shot back, ignoring the ache in his heart.

"I'm proud of you son, mighty proud."

By the time Joshua had become a young man, he was a self-assured, steady person. "You're in control; you're in charge. No doubt about it," Ezra beamed at his son. "You don't flinch at the sight of pain. You don't wear your heart on your sleeve like—" Ezra paused, pointed to Suzanna, and whispered, "like your mother there. I'm proud of you, Josh."

Yes, proud he was; and proud was Joshua of Ezra's pride. How nice if the mutual sentiment had gone on forever. How nice indeed. Unfortunately, it didn't. Ezra's pride in Joshua vanished the day Ezra died of a heart attack. Now Joshua's strength was really put to the test. In the weeks that followed, Suzanna cried and cried, but not Joshua. There were no tears. Absolutely none.

"So controlled," his friends remarked.

"Bearing up under it with such grace," his relatives commented.

"A son his dad would be proud of," the neighbors agreed.

A son his dad could be proud of? *His* dad? His dad was gone. He wasn't there.

But Joshua was there with the stiff upper lip, half waiting for Ezra's approving words. He waited and waited. Yet Ezra didn't show. In the weeks and months that followed, Josh waited—waited without tears as had been expected and taken for granted. But were there traces of anger to be seen in those eyes devoid of tears?

"Looks a little angry to me," a friend detected.

"You must be mistaken," a second objected. "Not our Josh. He's just like his dad. In control and always will be." Undoubtedly, the second friend had to be right. After all, what possible reason could there be for Josh to be angry?

But one thing certainly couldn't be mistaken. Joshua had stopped doing anything: no eating, no working, no exercising. He took to his bed. He didn't move—at all. Suzanna couldn't get him up. His neighbors and friends couldn't rouse him. No one could do anything.

"He's dead. He's dead," Suzanna cried. "Or he might as well be. What can we do?" Nothing but carry him outside on a stretcher and have him breathe in the fresh air. And that's what they did. They placed Joshua on a stretcher and moved him about the city. This they did for days. But the fresh air didn't rescue Joshua from the land of the living dead. Suzanna's tears flowed as freely for Joshua as they had for Ezra. Wringing her hands, she wondered what she could do for him.

LETDOWNS

One afternoon as Suzanna and her neighbors carried the stretcher bearing Joshua, a young man came up to them and bade them set down the stretcher. Suzanna recognized him as the young rabbi Jesus.

"Sir," she said, "how can you help my son?"

"By doing what he can't do for himself," Jesus replied.

"And what is that, sir?" Suzanna pleaded.

"Leave the two of us alone for a while," Jesus said without answering her question. "Please, and take your neighbors with you," he added gently.

Suzanna had no idea what Jesus would do, but she trusted him. So she and the others walked across the street and stood as they curiously eyed what Jesus would do. What he did shocked them. Stretching his whole body alongside of Joshua's, he began wailing loudly toward the heavens, "Why have you left me? How could you do this?" Over and over he cried, "Why have you left me? How could you do this?" As the wailing grew louder, Jesus' whole body heaved and his words were frequently punctuated with sobs. After about ten minutes of this, Suzanna noticed Joshua's body beginning to stir. Within seconds it started to heave in tandem with Jesus' body. To her amazement Joshua also cried out, "Why have you left me? How could you do this?" Over and over Joshua's mournful intonations were accompanied by Jesus' wailing.

"He's moving," Suzanna cried to the others. "He's moving. He's alive. He's alive."

Then they saw Jesus get up from alongside of Joshua and stretch out both hands toward Joshua as he firmly but gently enjoined him, "Young man, I bid you get up." Slowly Joshua sat up and then got to his feet. When he stood facing Jesus, Jesus placed his hands on

Joshua's shoulders, smiled, and told him, "Joshua, today you have become a man." Thereupon he looked at Suzanna, who by this time had hurried back from the other side of the street. "Here is your son. He is alive."

The neighbors who followed Suzanna began to praise God. "A great prophet has risen among us. God has visited his people." And that day this was the report that spread about him throughout Judea and the surrounding country.

Reflection

*Deep down I'm nobody
because you died and let me down.*

If someone close to us dies, it is appropriate to grieve: acknowledge the loss and say goodbye. Failure to grieve can bring on severe depression, especially if the death holds as much significance as Joshua's father's death held for Joshua.

In "Becoming A Man," Joshua faced a twofold loss. Besides losing his father, he also lost the sole source of his self-esteem. To a certain extent, Joshua suffered depression because of the male image his father modeled, an image that counseled repression of feelings and a stiff upper lip in the presence of suffering. "Real men aren't supposed to cry." This assumption governed his life so completely he couldn't express any kind of feelings for his father's death. But another assumption had also been operative, namely, that his worth was completely dependent on another. Joshua valued himself only if his father were proud of him.

Is it any wonder, then, that Joshua became depressed? His losses were staggering and he found them impossible to deal with. Why? Because reviewing the assumptions that governed his life would mean reassessing the father whom he idealized, the central component in his self-identity. That in turn would be like attacking himself. How then did he respond to his father's death? Simulating it, he sunk into a deep depression.

Jesus responded to Joshua's depression by evoking long buried feelings of anger, resentment, and sorrow. Frequently, depressed people harbor negative as well as positive feelings toward the persons they love the most, but because they fear a loss of connection with the other they repress their feelings. Unless and until the feelings are expressed, depressed people remain depressed. In "Becoming A Man," Joshua had to confront his illusions about himself, his father, and mankind and consciously mourn their loss before he could actually become a man himself.

When someone dies or a relationship comes to an end, as in divorce, can we let go of the other and acknowledge the loss? Does our difficulty in letting go point to the other's having been the major source of our self-esteem? Is it possible that in our moments of profound loneliness we also begin to experience our selves as separate and unique, as persons existing in our own right? Can we believe that someone's death need not leave us feeling like nobody forever, but can be the occasion for discovering we really are somebody?

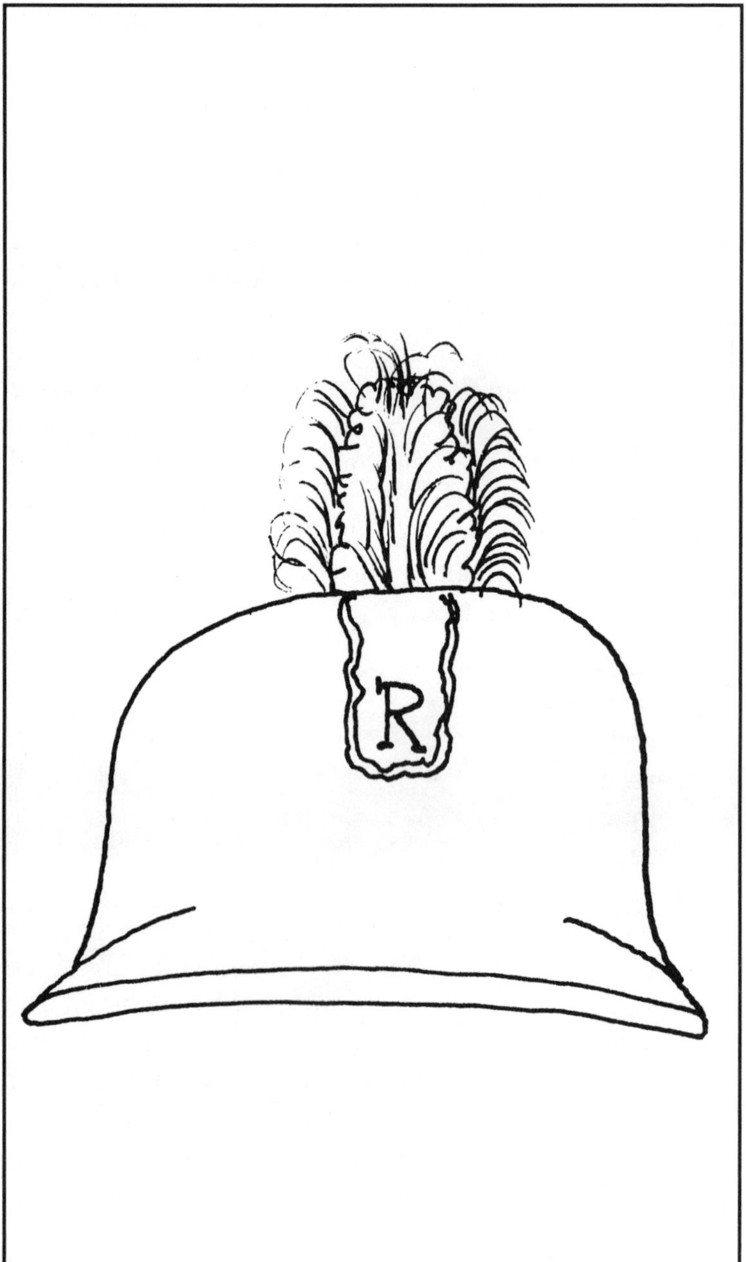

R

ORDERS

Luke 7:2-4: A centurion had a servant he held in high regard, who was at that moment sick to the point of death. When he heard about Jesus he sent some Jewish elders to him, asking him to come and save the life of his servant.

"Sandals!"
"Here, sir!"
"Tunic!"
"Here, sir!"
"Helmet!"
"Here, sir!"
"Good!"

The two of them went through the same routine every morning. Marcus gave the orders and Eli carried them out. Marcus' word of approval concluded the ritual, and the day was underway. For Marcus it was simply the beginning of another day, but for Eli Marcus' seal of approval was the high point of the day. Unfortunately, because of Marcus' busy schedule, this morning ritual was the only time Eli ordinarily saw Marcus.

Eli, now twelve years old, had been orphaned a year earlier when his only living relative, his mother, died of a heart condition. Since she had been a servant in the centurion's household, Marcus assumed responsibility for Eli's upbringing. Some of the servants guessed Marcus' decision to keep the boy was an attempt to fill the void created by the tragic drowning deaths of his wife and young son three years earlier. Other servants dismissed this reasoning. "How," they wondered, "could a man of his rank want a servant boy as a substitute for his own son?" As a matter of fact, Marcus' cool, soldierly exterior made it difficult for anyone to know what he felt or wanted. A fair man, yes. A good man, yes. But what he actually felt no one knew.

Although Eli looked up to Marcus as a father, he was very much aware of the social distance between them. As a result, he was anxious not to show any affection toward Marcus, nor did he feel he had any right to expect affection in return. Instead he had to be satisfied with the few words of commendation and the occasional pat on the head he received for helping ready Marcus for the day. This arrangement continued unchanged for several months. Then, one morning after Marcus had bestowed his stamp of approval, Eli blurted, "Do you really mean it?"

Puzzled, Marcus looked down. "Do I really mean what?"

Realizing he was now engaging his master in a conversation that moved beyond their routine dialogue, Eli stammered, "Do, do, do you really mean what I did was good?"

"Good?" Trying to recall what he had just said to Eli, Marcus scratched his head and then, with a look of recognition, nodded "Oh yes! You did a good job. Yes indeed." Then Marcus took a step toward the boy, placed a hand on his head, and said softly, "Eli, you remind me a lot of my own—" He stopped abruptly, cleared his throat and continued brusquely, "Oh, and before I forget, Eli, there's a new boy coming in today. For the next month or so, he will be doing for me what you are doing. It's time you take on a job with a little more responsibility."

Eli's heart sank as he tried to fight back the tears. "But I, I...," he stammered. Eli wanted to say, "I want to stay here with you," but he couldn't. Once Marcus had given an order, that was it. There was no room for discussion or compromise. It was no wonder he ran an efficient household, not to mention an elite corps of Roman soldiers.

"Go now," Marcus ordered Eli. "I need to be alone." The conversation was over.

During the days that followed, Eli assumed more responsibilities, but without Marcus there to utter that one encouraging word, Eli became less and less inclined to carry out his duties and more and more disposed to linger in bed. When he finally did get up, he moved listlessly through the huge building. Finally Eli didn't even bother to get out of bed and stopped eating altogether.

As Eli lay in bed one morning, Marcus peeked in the doorway, marshaled his energies, and strode into the room unobserved. For a minute he stood looking warmly at Eli. Then he advanced to the foot of the bed and spoke matter-of-factly. "Eli, you've got to get better. You're needed in the house. The other servants say you do a great job," he added. Eli stared at the ceiling. He wasn't interested in what a great job others thought he did. "Of course, I can vouch for that," Marcus continued. "You always performed well for me," he reflected as he stared off into space.

Eli winced at the words "performed well." "Is that all I mean to him?" he thought. Eli didn't stir. But his eyes followed Marcus, who now paced the room distractedly. Marcus drew nearer as if to sit on the bed or touch the boy on the arm, but he stopped himself and instead half waved, half saluted.

"Eli, I shall be back. I think there is someone who can help you, someone who commands the respect and attention of many persons here and in the countryside. If he's that kind of a man, he certainly has my trust." Eli didn't particularly care about being helped. At this point he didn't care much about anything.

Hours later, Marcus reentered his room. He said nothing but looked at Eli as if he anticipated some change in Eli's health. Eli paid little attention to Marcus until Marcus sat down near his bed and slowly extended his hand to Eli's forehead, cheeks, and finally his wrists. Almost involuntarily he gently stroked the boy's hair and then took his small hands into his own. Tears began to form in Marcus' eyes as he drew nearer to Eli. He lifted him up from his pillows and cradled him in his arms. "Eli, I've missed you more than I realized. Eli, I love you like my own son."

Marcus' words were life to Eli. He snuggled closely to Marcus and whispered, "Do you mean it? Really?"

"Oh yes, I do," Marcus answered as he held the boy tightly.

Eli put his arms around Marcus. "I feel better. Could I have something to eat?"

"We'll both have something to eat," Marcus smiled, "and then let's go and thank someone who can get orders carried out a lot faster than I can."

Reflection

*Deep down I'm nobody
because something in me died since you left.*

In "Orders" Eli's loss is evident and his subsequent depression understandable, given the fact that his sense of well-being was so dependent on Marcus' word of approval. What isn't so evident is the effect the loss of his wife and son had on Marcus. We know little about Marcus. What we do know is he didn't appear to be aware of what Eli felt. Like many people whom we know, Marcus seemed oblivious of what was going on inside himself. More given to action than reflection, Marcus might have attempted conducting business as usual after their deaths. Did he acknowledge their loss and grieve for them? Equally important, did Marcus grieve for himself?

The feeling of emptiness that accompanies depression is often a reference to a lost dimension of the Self. When someone dies, something of us dies as well, and we grieve not only for losing the other but for losing something of ourselves in the passing of the other. Therefore a depressed person must grieve for himself or herself no less than for the person who has gone. This is a remote preparation for the emergence of new aspects of the Self over a period of time.

But such letting go may be particularly difficult. It may feel as if we are betraying the other by saying good-bye. This vague sense of betrayal in saying goodbye accounts for us wanting to say and do what the deceased would have said or done if he or she were still alive. It also accounts for holding on to clothes, books, etc., that the deceased possessed. The feeling of betrayal and the accompanying guilt may be too great an expense to pay and so the survivor continues with the illusion that nothing has changed.

Hopefully in time a person may incorporate in memory the person who is no longer physically present. Then letting go becomes possible because of the transformation of the other's presence in a new way. This is a way of establishing continuity with what is lost and now past without being paralyzed by the loss and unable to live in the present and future.

When we have to say good-bye, do we realize we have to say good-bye not only to the other but to something of ourselves as well? Can we recognize that the emptiness we feel isn't purely absence but is also a space necessary for something new to be born? Can we finally let go of feeling like nobody because we feel the other left and took us along?

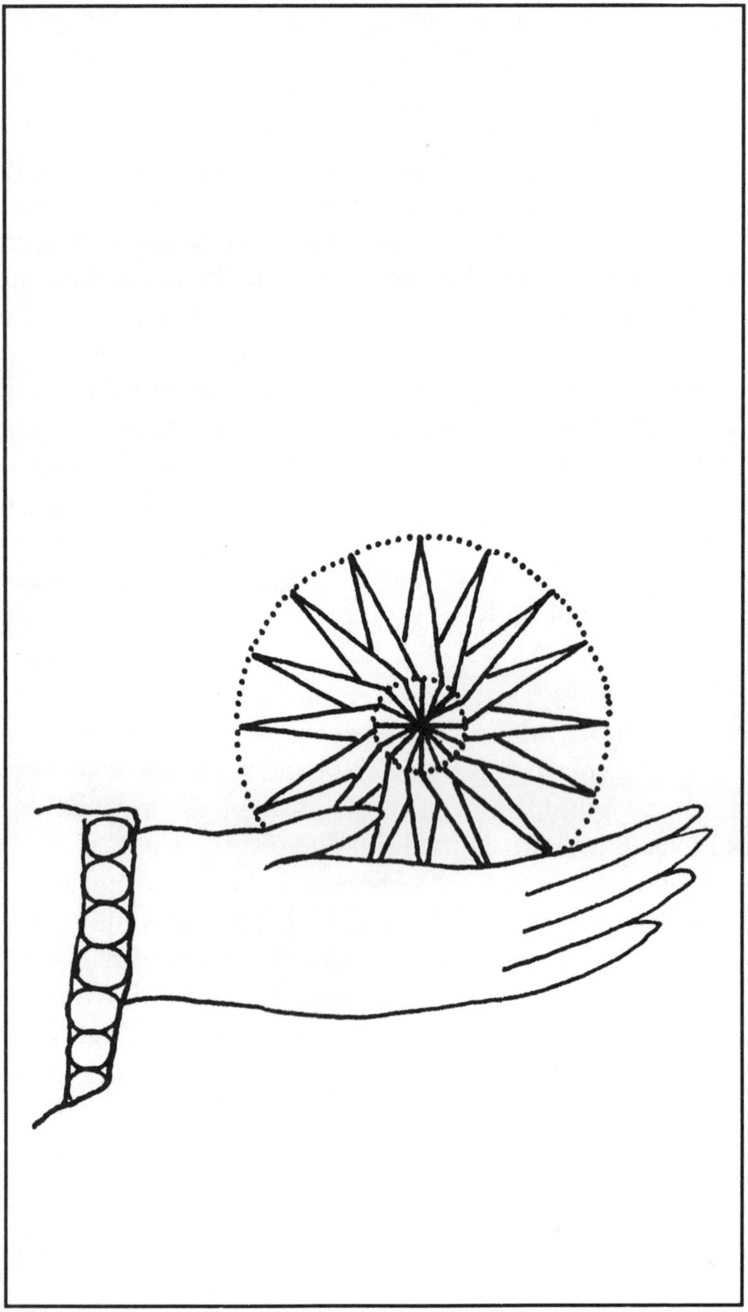

SIMEON

Luke 2:25-37: There lived in Jerusalem at the time a certain man named Simeon. He was just and pious, and awaited the consolation of Israel, and the Holy Spirit was upon him. It was revealed to him by the Holy Spirit that he would not experience death until he had seen the Anointed of the Lord.

Every day he went to the temple to pray. Simeon told himself he would not end his days in darkness. He couldn't explain this belief. Nor did he know whether this was what he wanted to believe or needed to believe. The point is he did believe this.

Of course, if anyone had reason to believe otherwise, it was Simeon himself. He had had more than his share of tragedies. It was bad enough when two of his sons drowned after their fishing boat had gone down in a storm. It seemed more than he could bear. Each day after the accident he would walk along the shore and search the sea with his eyes. It was as though he were expecting his sons to come home—as though they had never drowned. When it finally began to sink in that they would not come back, he felt an ache in his heart that he had never felt before. The ache was there for

LETDOWNS

days and weeks and months. Simeon could have been swallowed up by his grief, but this he would not permit. Instead, he let the aching of his own heart draw him to be with other fathers whose sons had shared a similar fate at sea.

What he couldn't have anticipated was the fate of his youngest son, his dearest son. Reuben was only ten when his brothers had drowned. He was slight of build and pale looking. Simeon thought it was just a matter of time before Reuben put on more weight. But he didn't. And before he was fifteen, Reuben deteriorated in health, losing rather than gaining weight. As Simeon saw his son lose more and more weight, so did his hopes for his son begin to disappear. The day Reuben died, Simeon wanted to die. Far easier to die than to bear the weight of so much sorrow, so much grief. At least with the drowning of his two other sons, he could point to the storm to explain why they had drowned. When he picked up the dead Reuben in his arms, Simeon could only shake his head. He could find no reason for this, no explanation. He had so many questions and no answers, only the dead silence and darkness that covered his soul like a pall.

For days and months Simeon would pass the door of his son's room and feel the aching in his heart. Yet, even in the midst of all this suffering, he would not give up his belief that he would not end his days in darkness. As with the aching in his heart that he felt for his two other sons, Simeon let this aching open him up even more to the others. For he began to see and notice much more than he had before what this man or that woman was going through in similar tragedies. And just as he began to see and notice more the suffering of others, so too did others come to notice how Simeon bore his own grief. The way he bore the grief in his heart drew the grief-stricken to share more deeply the ache they carried in their hearts. Thus, they knew he could be present to their suffering even though he couldn't explain the why of it all.

As the years rolled by, Simeon continued to believe that he would not end his days in darkness, and he continued to come to the temple to express that belief. That belief seemed to be particularly strong one summer day as he walked into the temple. There were few persons there: a handful of tourists and a family of three—a young man, his wife, and their newborn baby. As though they knew he was the one to perform the ritual purification of the mother and the child, they gave him a look of recognition. At that moment, something within Simeon stirred. It was an experience of light, light that flooded his soul. And the more he looked at the child, the more he felt the light within. By the time the young man approached Simeon and asked him to perform the ceremony of purification, Simeon was already reaching out to take the child in his arms. The child tugged at Simeon's beard and as their eyes met, Simeon realized that not only his days but the days of others would not end in darkness. With a smile that crossed his face and captured the light of his soul, Simeon held the child high and said:

"Now, Master you can dismiss your servant in peace; you have fulfilled your word.

For my eyes have witnessed your saving deed displayed for all the peoples to see:

A revealing light to the Gentiles, the glory of your people Israel."

LETDOWNS

Simeon would have preferred to have stopped there but he could not; there was more. There always was. He turned to the young mother and said:

"This child is destined to be the downfall and the rise of many in Israel,

and to be a sign that will be opposed—and you yourself shall be pierced with a sword—so that the thoughts of many hearts may be laid bare."

The young woman, surprised at Simeon's words, studied his face and wondered how any suffering of hers could prompt others to disclose the grief in their own hearts. Simeon gave her no answer, but she suspected the old man knew firsthand what he was talking about. While she momentarily shuddered over what lay in store for her, she also took consolation from the light on Simeon's face that the darkness would not triumph. Light would. Simeon believed that right along and the light in his face justified that belief. He had not ended his days in darkness.

Reflection

Deep down I'm nobody because my children left me.

    Three sons were lost to Simeon, and with them the illusion that children will always outlive their parents. Anyone who is a parent or knows a parent who has lost a son or daughter regards the situation as somehow dark and "unnatural." However, Simeon's losses generated the belief that he would not die in darkness. And it was this belief that sustained him for years. Some might call Simeon's belief yet another illusion. After all, what makes belief any different from all other illusions or myths?
    Generally, assumptions or illusions say, "This is the way things are; this is the way it has to be." Assumptions are what we take for granted. Otherwise they wouldn't be assumptions! But Simeon's belief was open-ended. His confidence that he would not die in darkness never provided a blueprint for how he would experience the light. Illusions help us think we can manage the unmanageable, whereas the kind of belief Simeon had inclines us toward trusting that The Unmanageable will manage us kindly.
    Simeon's belief did more than guide him into the future. It provided hope for others. His suffering opened him to embrace others; out of the death of his sons and his disillusionment and depression, he brought life to others. This is an important point.
    Too much literature on depression focuses on people withdrawing and being absorbed by their suffering. While this is true in many instances, it is also true that people can be depressed because they are extremely sensitive to the brutality, stupidity, and insensitivity around them. Consequently, their profound sadness

engages them in a greater commitment to what is happening in their world. One can think of people like Dag Hammarskjold and Simone Weil, who suffered from depression but didn't allow it to isolate them from their world; rather it plunged them ever more deeply into it.

Simeon's loss, then, was his world's gain. We see similar patterns occurring in divorce groups, widow/widower groups, etc., where people come together to support one another out of—not in spite of—having suffered loss and depression.

Do we trust that the emptiness created by another's death can be transformed into the space where we receive others who are going through their own grieving? Or do we despair by withdrawing forever because we feel we are nobody with nothing to give to anybody?

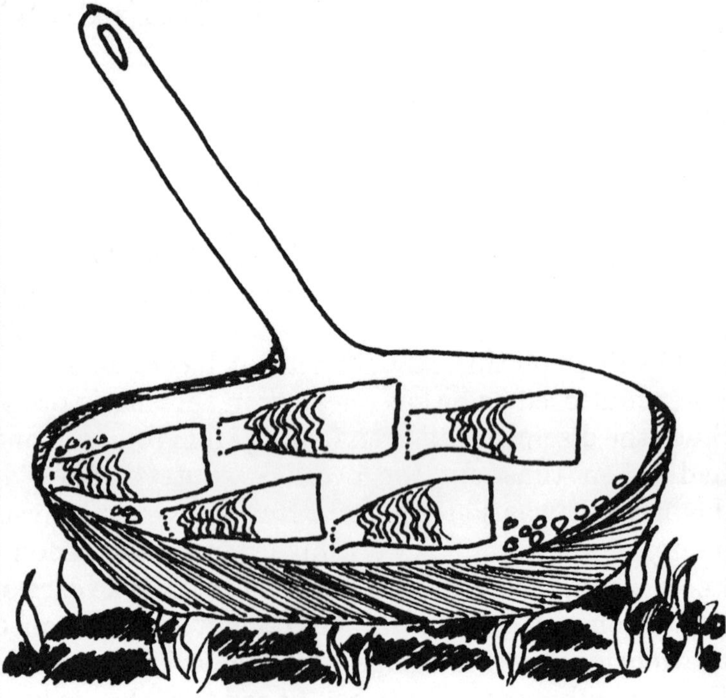

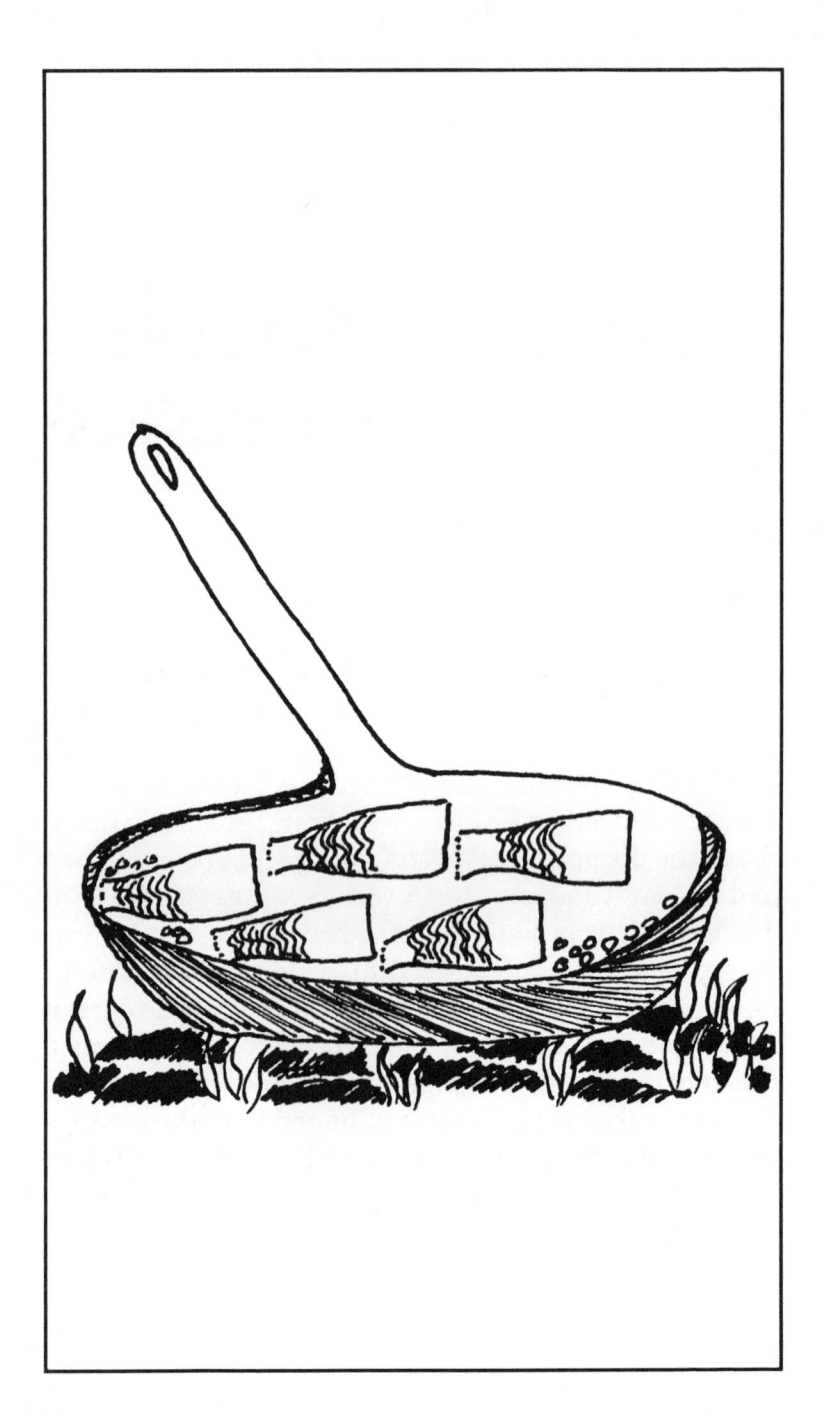

PETER'S UNFINISHED BUSINESS

John 21:15: When they had eaten their meal, Jesus said to Simon Peter, "Simon, son of John, do you love me more than these?" "Yes, Lord," he said, "you know that I love you."

"I can't go on this way. Something has to be done," Peter muttered as he sat uneasily in the boat's prow. Since the disciples had been fishing all night, each one had taken time out for a quick shuteye. Now at daybreak it was Peter's turn. But whenever he was alone, he was haunted by unfinished business. "I don't know when, where, or how, but I've got to take care of it. It's going to be painful," he thought as he watched the morning waves nudge the boat ever so gently. Earlier in the week, Peter had hoped to make amends when Jesus made a surprise visit to their meeting place. "No, it wouldn't have worked," he reflected. "Too many people around—no privacy!"

His thoughts were interrupted when he heard a voice hailing him from the shore, "Have you caught anything yet?"

"What was that?" Peter yelled back.

"I say, have you caught any fish yet?"

"Have we caught any fish? No, I'm afraid not."

"Then try the starboard side. Lower your nets on the starboard side."

"Yes, yes," Peter answered sharply. "Maybe he sees something we don't. At this point anything is worth a try." He stood and called out to the others, "Lower the nets on the starboard side." Startled by Peter's unexpected order, they looked skeptically at one another, but they, too, were ready to try anything. No sooner had they lowered them down than the nets began loading up with an incredible haul of fish. As Peter and the others retrieved their nets, he laughed, "Besides myself, there's only one other person who knows where to catch the fish like this and that's—!" His eyes widening, he exclaimed "Jesus?" Scanning the shoreline, he spotted the stranger and recognizing him cried, "It is Jesus! It's Jesus!" Throwing a pair of shorts on his naked body, he plunged into the water and swam for shore.

Peter was out of breath as he staggered like a drunken man onto the beach. "You were right! You were right!" he gasped as he straggled toward Jesus. "I should have known it was you." They laughed together as they used to laugh before. It was a grand reunion as they embraced one another warmly. Or was it? As the laughter subsided, Peter felt an awkward silence grow. "It's not the same with us," he thought. "Now is the time. I've got to discuss it."

"Jesus," Peter began nervously.

Peter's Unfinished Business

"Not now," Jesus raised a hand and seemed to mirror Peter's discomfort. "There'll be time. Right now, just go and get some of those fish you caught. We want to eat, don't we?"

"Sure, Jesus, sure. I'll get us the best of the haul," Peter deferred, not a little resentful that Jesus hadn't treated his concern with more urgency, hadn't seemed interested in getting things settled.

Around the campfire it was like old times, almost. But Jesus was somehow different. Certainly he hadn't changed his style of preparing the fish. And he had gotten the same kind of bread with the hard crust they all liked so well. But he had changed. No one mentioned it, but they all knew.

No one seemed more aware of that and more ill at ease than Peter as they began cleaning up the campsite. In the early excitement of the catch, Peter's recognition of Jesus, and their breakfast together, the pain of the unfinished business had been temporarily muted, but it was back now as he fussed with the nets. Peter knew he had to deal with it.

"Jesus," he said as he walked over to the shore where Jesus was stooped over washing a pan. "We have to talk now!"

Jesus averted his eyes. "Of course, Peter, of course." He took more time than necessary finishing his task and set the pan on the old boat. Then the two began walking along the shore beyond the campsite. For the longest time neither of them spoke. Then Jesus stopped, looked back toward the others in the distance, and said to Peter, "Do you love me more than these?"

Peter wasn't prepared for that question. He had his own business to discuss, and now Jesus raised this question. "Of course. Yes, I love you," Peter answered matter-of-factly.

There was silence. Now Jesus turned, looked directly at Peter, and searched his eyes carefully. "Did you hear me? Are you listening?"

Connecting with Jesus' earnest tone, Peter answered carefully, "Yes."

Speaking slowly and deliberately, Jesus repeated, "Simon Peter, do you love me?"

"Is he playing a game with me?" Peter wondered. "Haven't I just answered his question. After all these years, he asks this question. He should know. He should know?" Peter caught himself. "Should he? I do have this habit of saying one thing and doing the other. Habit? Huh! What a clean word for betrayal! And that's exactly what I need to talk about."

Answering in a subdued and almost halting voice, Peter answered as carefully and deliberately as Jesus had asked the question. "You know that I love you." Peter knew he had answered from the heart and hoped that Jesus would know that as well.

Jesus said nothing; they resumed their walk in silence. Then, quite unexpectedly, Jesus asked yet another time, "Do you love me?" His voice was uncertain and ached with the need for reassurance.

Peter was taken by surprise, but he wasn't hurt, just surprised. Peter caught the strong feeling behind Jesus' question. He began to realize Jesus had his own unfinished business: a deep need to be assured that what Peter had done he hadn't meant and would never do again. "Hmmmm," he thought, "What can I say? No matter how I answer, there'll always be room for doubt. Just like I often doubt he can have forgiven me!" Tears forming in his eyes, Peter embraced his friend. Painfully aware of how he had once denied Jesus with words, he spoke as earnestly as he could, "You know all things; you know I love you!"

Peter felt he finally told Jesus what he had so sincerely longed to tell him. "Surely I can do no more," he thought. But there was more, much more.

Jesus' own eyes welled up as he spelled out what lay ahead for Peter. "I tell you Peter. When you were young, you girded yourself and walked where you would; but when you are old, you will stretch out your hands, and another will gird you and carry you where you do not wish to go." Having said these words, Jesus placed his hand on Peter's shoulder and said, "Come, follow me."

Their business was far from finished yet.

Reflection

*Deep down I'm nobody
because my friend let me down.*

In "Peter's Unfinished Business," Peter was aware of his shadow, and his unfinished business was to bring some kind of closure to his betrayal. He wanted to make amends. Obviously, Peter's acknowledgment of what he had done was an important step, but it was only the first step. What the rest of the story tells us is that bringing closure to something so profound as a betrayal is not accomplished by an act of the will. People who have been betrayed can't dismiss it merely because their perceived betrayer wants to kiss and make up. We notice a certain reserve, a tentativeness in Jesus' approach to Peter. They embraced, but there was also a distance that couldn't be overcome through remembering the good old days and cracking jokes around the fire. And Peter's later assurances and reassurances of love and fidelity couldn't entirely remove the distance between them.

Perhaps there is a lesson for us here. Both betrayer and betrayed need to suffer that distance consciously and not yield to the notion that it must be overcome in a day, week, month, or year. Maintaining an awareness of whatever distance exists is a testimony to the undeniable change in the relationship. Now, "maintaining an awareness" doesn't refer to the betrayed forever posturing as the victim of an inconsolable hurt. Rather, it means in the first place permitting the betrayal to stand for what it is: a painful reminder of the expectations and naive trust we bring to relationships and the frequent if not inevitable letdown such trust engenders. Secondly, it means living in the hope that God, not we, will transform the wounded relationship into something new and more mature. What might be some components of a more mature relationship?

Eventually the betrayed might begin to see a complicity in the betrayal, for as the introduction noted, setups result not only from what is done to us but what we are willing to have done to us, consciously or unconsciously. For example, if we had considered ourselves the innocent partner in a broken marriage, might we come to see that our neglect or indifference may have played a part in the breakdown? Did we assume a common understanding without ever actively trying to understand our partner? If we ourselves in no way complied with the betrayer (e.g., as childhood victims of abuse), nevertheless we might begin to see how much our parents may have been victimized by their parents, and how we may be engaged in victimizing our children.

Another component in a more mature relationship is the recognition of the limits of promises in any relationship. We promise to love, honor, and obey, or we promise to keep a secret, professionally or otherwise. We say we will never go back on our word, just as Peter had sworn never to betray Jesus. But frequently promises are made rashly or by people with very little self-understanding.

In all these instances, time is needed to integrate the meaning of betrayal. Any attempt to gloss over or prematurely forgive a betrayal, or even to seek forgiveness for a betrayal, might lessen whatever meaning there is in it.

When we feel like nobody because a friend has let us down, reflecting on this story and reflection may be helpful, but this doesn't mean we will feel better about ourselves. Reflection or analysis is no substitute for going through what we must go through. The challenge is in letting the betrayal be, neither minimizing nor maximizing what has happened.

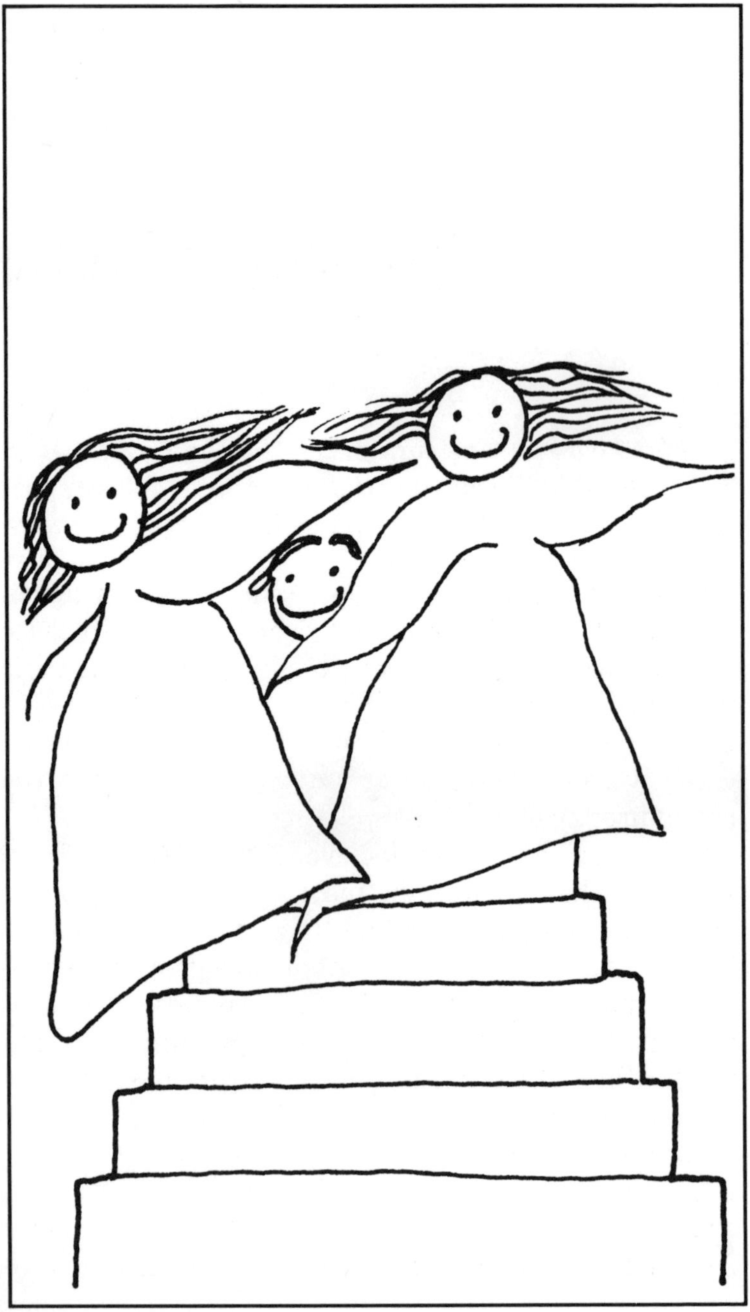

UP AND DOWN

Matthew 2:9: The star which they had observed at its rising went ahead of them until it came to a standstill over the place where the child was.

Up and down. Up and down. Manny was very upset, very upset. In fact, he hadn't been so upset since he and his wife had gone into bankruptcy when their furniture business folded. Here they were in this fleabitten, cockroach-ridden Times Square Hotel with all those weirdos going up and down the stairs to the room directly above theirs.

He was upset because he never thought he and Ruth would be sharing a lumpy mattress on a secondhand bed when they had once had their own heated waterbeds He was upset because instead of eating off expensive china, he was eating off chipped plates with faded designs. He was also upset because he and Ruth had worked hard, real hard, spent all their time running the business even to the point of frequently ignoring others—the children, relatives, friends.

Of course, Manny and Ruth had intended to get around to those needs, but the business always came first. This was their first concern; it was serious business. They hadn't time for any foolishness. But now as Manny sat on the lumpy mattress, he thought of all that time, all that effort. And for what? It wasn't fair! One bad year in the business and they had lost everything. Everything! And how embarrassing to have been thrown out of their Park Avenue condo!

And now here they were sitting in their room, with the crazies going up and down, up and down the stairs. Who were they, anyhow? Where did they come from? What were they doing up there? The first time Manny had opened the door, he saw three guys dressed up in long, flowing, colorful robes, and they were climbing the stairs. "Fags!" he said to himself. What right did they have to be coming there? Well, he had to admit this was probably headquarters for them; they had more of a right to be there than he. After all, this wasn't the condo on Park Avenue!

However, the next time he opened the door after he heard a strange, shuffling sound, he thought he had every right to put his foot down. There on the steps were two men hauling three mangy-looking sheep up the steps to the room above. "Hey you, what the hell is going on up there?" Manny yelled after them. The two men just smiled and invited him to come up. "Yeh," Manny thought to himself. He wanted to yell back "Not with you perverts!" but he held back and simply said under his breath, "Not on your life, not on your life," and closed the door. He turned his attention to Ruth, who was beside herself and had already started to pack the few belongings they had. "No, Ruth, we haven't anywhere else to go," Manny said with a quiet despair.

And even as he said that he heard more noise—up and down, up and down. He hesitated to open the door, but he mustered up enough courage, braced himself, and opened the door slowly. When he peeked out, he saw four people dressed in white gowns trimmed with what appeared to be white Christmas tree lights going on and off. The four were making their way up the stairs. Manny had to ask the question even though he already knew the answer he'd get. "And who are you?"

"Who do we look like?" one of the robed figures replied.

"Angels?" Manny answered feebly.

"You got it," another white-robed figure answered as all of them beckoned Manny to follow them into the room where all the others had gone. Manny couldn't resist. He left the room while Ruth looked on in horror.

Ruth was frozen in place for what seemed an eternity. Manny still hadn't returned by the time she was able to move again. Should she call the police? No, there was no time for that. She would simply have to go up the stairs and find Manny herself. She got out of the chair, walked slowly through the open door, and climbed the stairs cautiously. Ruth hesitated as she stood in front of the door to the room where all the others had entered. Slowly she opened the door and peeked in.

There in the room were the three men dressed in long colorful robes, two shabbily dressed shepherds, three sheep, four angels, and a young man and woman with a small child sitting in the woman's lap. The child was smiling at everyone in the room. They all smiled back at the child as well as at one another. (The sheep were grinning because sheep can't quite smile, hence the expression, "a sheepish grin"). What were they all smiling about, she wondered. They weren't doing anything, these crazy people, just smiling and enjoying themselves.

Then she panicked. She had forgotten about Manny. Where was Manny? Her eyes swept the room again, and she caught a glimpse of him between two of the angels. And Manny was smiling! No wonder she hadn't seen him at first; he hadn't smiled in years! He had never had the time to smile and sit with other people as he was doing now. No, the only time he sat was when he was demonstrating how comfortable a sofa was to a potential customer.

Of course, the light was very bright; that was another reason she hadn't at first seen him. Then she realized there were no lamps in the room, nor windows. Where was the light coming from? She didn't know. All she knew was that she was aware of people smiling and of intense light. "Aha!" she said as she began to put two and two together. "Smiling and light, smiling and light. Yes, that's it! The light is coming from all this smiling!" Ruth said in amazement. Then she began to smile and the light in the room became even more intense.

The darkness in that drab room was dispelled by the simple fact that these people had sat down to relax and smile in one another's company. Ruth decided not to interrupt Manny. She liked what she saw in the room and she wanted to be a part of it. So she went and sat down between the two shepherds and the grinning sheep. And she smiled as she had never smiled before.

Reflection

Deep down I'm nobody because my work is gone.

Manny and Ruth were workaholics: people addicted to their work with no time for anything else. Their captivation was so complete they could not live out other aspects of their lives, until, that is, they went bankrupt and experienced disillusionment. The letdown left them disgusted about themselves, their work, and their future. However, it also opened up a space in their lives so they could experience something other than their work.

The chaotic, crazy, unstructured Times Square area of New York mirrored the chaotic period of their lives. Precisely because it was chaotic, there was the possibility for a new vision to emerge. Manny had free time to follow the strange, motley assortment of characters up the stairs to the room above their own. These marginal, strange characters crowded into a room and sat on the floor as they exchanged smiles with a small child on his mother's lap. Manny, too, was free to sit (something Ruth remembered him doing only as part of his job in the furniture business) and experience a contemplative, work-free, relaxed dimension of himself, which he had never known before. When Ruth joined him, she, too, got in touch with a dimension of herself that her addiction to work had prevented her from noticing. And light was born out of their disillusionment in that upper room.

Only when we are disillusioned and the spell is broken are we freed up to see and celebrate dimensions of life that our enchantment did not permit us to see. The energy previously invested and tied up in the object of our addiction is now available for us to reinvest in other realities. Of course, the possibility exists that we shall find another object in which we once more lose ourselves and create another idol.

Can we discover ways to reinvest our energies that enable us to be more available to one another and creation? Or do we content ourselves with thinking we are nobody because our work is gone?

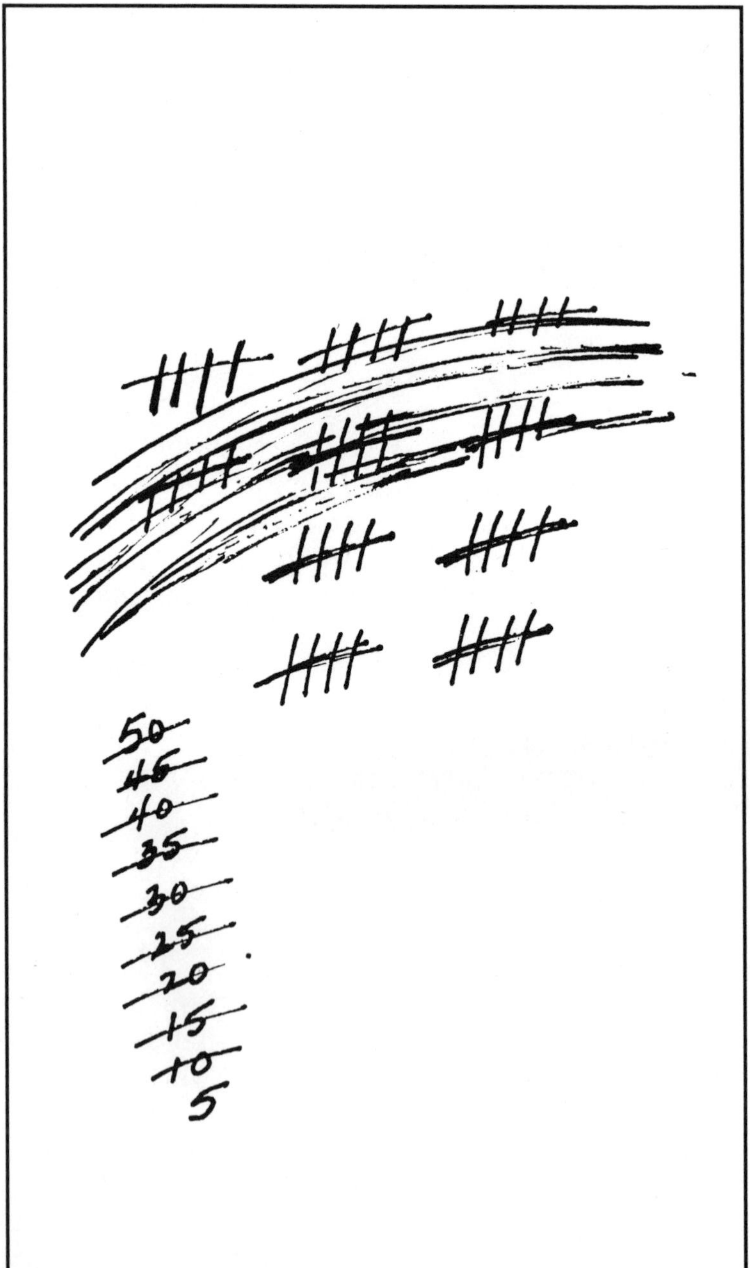
50
45
40
35
30
25
20
15
10
5

THE LAST REQUEST

Genesis 18:22-23: While the two men walked on farther, toward Sodom, the LORD remained standing before Abraham. Then Abraham drew nearer to him and said "Will you sweep away the innocent with the guilty?"

"Smoke! Smoke!" A scraggly-bearded pusher peddled his wares.

"Hey man, can you spare a couple of bucks? My mother's dying and I need money for medicine," slurred the booze-bleary derelict.

"Read all about it!" bellowed the vendor from his newsstand throne. "Mayor, city council, and judges deny dirty dealing!"

"I've had it with these people, Abe. They've had their day and now it's time for me to have mine." The Lord God was not in good humor that hot, humid afternoon as he and Abe walked warily down Sodom's infamous 8th Avenue. In fact, the Lord had all but decided to destroy the whole town because of what he saw that day. "We can't walk more than twenty feet without something— Oops!" The divine foreknowledge proved all too accurate as the Lord of Heaven and Earth slipped and almost fell in the dog-doo that graced his side of the walk.

Lest the Lord wreak his vengeance then and there, Abe hastened to place the incident in perspective. "Lord, we do have laws requiring pooper-scoopers and most of our citizens usually—"

"Yeh, yeh," the Lord muttered as he wiped the offending substance from the side of his heavenly loafer with a discarded copy of the local gossip column, *The Sodom Delight*. Straightening to his full height of seven feet and readjusting his tunic, the Omnipotent One found his divine nose smack up against the marquee of a theater that advertised a girlie show. The marquee left nothing to the imagination. It showed ten naked women, the Sodom Sisters, dancing and throwing popcorn to the customers.

"Abraham, Abraham, I thought nudity had gone out with Adam and Eve? What's this all about?"

"I can't tell you based on firsthand knowledge, Lord, but from the picture I will wager it's more like a punishment to see them with their clothes off! So I wouldn't get too upset," Abe advised.

His logic limped, but it did seem to satisfy the Lord's curiosity except for one point. "Why the popcorn?" the Lord queried.

"Throwing popcorn just proves my point, Lord," Abe was thinking fast. "Since the Sodom Sisters aren't much to look at, the only way they can get customers to stay is to keep feeding them popcorn."

"Oh, is that it?" The Lord sounded skeptical, but he didn't think it worthwhile to pursue the matter; nor did he have time to consider it further since someone behind him tapped him on the shoulder.

The Last Request

"Hey big guy, how'd you like to have a little fun?" whispered a very ample-looking woman as she rubbed up to the Lord of Hosts and winked.

His right eyebrow arched, the Lord God glared at the pathetic woman whose orange fright wig practically touched his nose. "Fun? Do you think I created you to have fun in that way? Do you think I created anyone to have fun like that? Is that the only way you can have fun?" The Lord of Righteousness grew more indignant with each question as he assumed the classic right-hand-raised-to-the-heavens gesture.

"Hey big guy! Don't get so uptight!" The woman staggered back a step, drew Abe aside, and whispered, "What's with your friend? Does he think he's God or what? We've got places for people like him." Then she waddled off to lure another prospective customer.

Beads of perspiration broke out on Abe's brow as he attempted to cool the Lord's anger. "Clean-looking leotards, wouldn't you say, Lord?" he offered feebly.

"Clean-looking? Do you think I'm interested in clean leotards when she's...when she's...Well, do you?" The Lord's anger would not be assuaged. "What has happened to this town? Let's go back to your house. We'll see who is going to have fun!" Turning abruptly, the Lord strode down the street toward Abe's house in the suburbs.

Seeing that time was running out, Abe pleaded, "I know you're upset but please hear me out. Lord, um, Lord, could you slow down? I'm old and can hardly be expected to keep up with the Lord of Chariots."

Slowing down, the Lord apologized, "I'm sorry, Abe. I didn't mean to give you a hard time. But Sodom has got me so steamed up—not to mention Gomorrah! But don't get me started on that! Their time is up!" Pointing to a bench on a tree-lined street, the Creator of All Things invited Abe to rest. "Catch your breath and then we'll continue."

"Thanks Lord," Abe said as he plopped down. They both sat still for a minute. Finally, breathing more slowly, Abe presented his case. "Lord, will you sweep away the innocent with the guilty? Let's suppose there were fifty innocent people in Sodom. Would you wipe out the place rather than spare it for the sake of the fifty innocent people within it?"

Seeing the Lord was really giving his question consideration, Abe decided it might help to try a little flattery. Placing a hand on the Lord's arm to make certain he had his attention, he continued, "Far be it from you the Most Compassionate to do such a thing, to treat the innocent like the guilty!" Then Abe suddenly raised both arms in a dramatic gesture and cried, "Should not the Judge of All the World act with justice?"

Obviously moved by Abe's emotional appeal, the Lord acceded. "All right. If I find fifty innocent people in the city of Sodom, I will spare the whole place for their sake."

Abe decided to push his luck a little bit further. However, he knew he had to be careful not to seem pushy. Standing up and placing his hands behind his back, he swallowed hard, and eyes downcast mumbled, "See how I am presuming to speak to my Lord, though I am but dust and ashes!" Looking up out of the corner of his right eye, he waited for a green light from the Lord.

"Go ahead! Go ahead!" The Lord waved at him to continue.

The Last Request

Rushing his words quickly as possible, he asked "What if there are five less than fifty innocent people? Will you destroy the whole city because of those five?"

Not one to be outdone, the Lord jumped in, "I will not destroy it if I find forty-five there."

Thinking he was on a roll, Abe kept the momentum going, "What if only forty are found there?"

Permitting Abe to think he was on a roll, the Lord shot back, "I will forbear doing it for the sake of the forty."

Abe couldn't believe it was all going so easily. "Let not my Lord grow impatient if I go on. What if only thirty are found there?"

"I will forbear doing if I can find only thirty there."

By this time Abe had grown confident—too confident. Examining his nails casually, he continued, "Since I have thus dared to speak to my Lord, what if there are no more than twenty?"

Silence. Abe's composure dissolved. He realized he had presumed when he shouldn't have. Then the Lord spoke, "I will not destroy it for the sake of twenty."

"Phewww," Abe breathed a sigh of relief. He decided he had better go back to playing humble for this last request. "Please, let not my Lord grow angry if I speak up this last time. What if there are no more than ten there?"

The Lord relented. "For the sake of those ten I will not destroy the city."

Abe was about to wrap it up by inviting the Lord home for dinner when he found himself prompted to ask something he had had no intention of asking. "Lord, I know this is going to sound silly, but hear me out. Let's suppose there is no one, not one person who is innocent. Would you still destroy Sodom?"

LETDOWNS

The Lord hadn't expected this. "Abraham, what are you talking about? Why should I preserve the city if no one there is innocent? How merciful do you think I ought to be? What choice do I have?"

Abe was silent a minute. Then, quietly, he made what had to be the last request. "Don't you have someone back home who is innocent, whom you could send to us? Someone who could become one of us so it would be worth your while to save Sodom?"

The Lord God pondered this last request. He waited a long time before he spoke. "Yes, I have someone in mind. It will take a while before he comes, but it can be arranged. But Abraham, I don't think you realize the size of your request," the Lord God said, his voice a little raspy as his eyes moistened. "No, you don't realize it at all." Then the Lord God swallowed, smiled at Abe and asked, "Have you ever considered becoming a diplomat?"

Reflection
A Disillusioned God?

Whoever heard of God becoming disillusioned? And who would have thought the Incarnation would be the result of that disillusionment? Had God originally expected too much from his creatures? Was he so in love with the work of his hands that he was setting himself up for a letdown?

In "The Last Request," God was disillusioned and he wanted to destroy the work of his hands. Of course we can empathize with God. We've had occasion to want to destroy our own creations out of our disillusionment. Haven't we wanted to give up on a flawed relationship or to throw a son or daughter out of the house because of a mess the boy or girl had gotten into? Haven't we even contemplated giving up on ourselves because we think we have failed?

Abe was intelligent enough to see where God's disillusionment was moving Him, so he offered a solution: send someone over from God's side who would make it worthwhile for God to save everybody.

The suggestion was accepted. God decided to do it, but he let Abe know that his request demanded much of God, more than Abe could possibly understand. He would have to give up something of Himself in order for us to be acceptable once more.

Is God's action, which flowed from his disillusionment, a lesson and model for all of us? He sends what is his own, emptied of any claim to be more than human, and this is a signal to us that henceforth neither we nor God demand Godlike perfection of one another. What a marvelous paradox! That which is of

God became so emptied of God, but thereby became most acceptable to God and a model for our own way of being acceptable to one another and to God.

Setups lead us to see the holy pulsating in another person, and we are captivated. But letdowns prepare us to experience what is really holy in the other and in ourselves. And that is whatever is fully human.

Bibliography

Arieti, Silvano, and Jules Bemporad. *Severe and Mild Depression*. New York: Basic Books, 1978.

Assagioli, Roberto. "Self-Realization and Psychological Disturbances." *ReVision* (Winter-Spring 1986).

Bridges, William. *Transitions*. Reading, Massachusetts: Addison-Wesley Publishing Co., 1980.

Dittes, James E. *Male Predicament*. New York: Harper and Row Publishers, Inc., 1985.

Fairchild, Roy W. *Finding Hope Again: A Guide to Counseling the Depressed*. New York: Harper and Row Publishers, Inc., 1980.

Firman, John, and James Vargiu. "Dimensions of Growth." *Synthesis* 3-4, pp. 59-120

Fitzgerald, Constance, O.C.D. "Impasse and the Dark Night" in *Living With Apocalypse*, ed. Tilden H. Edwards. San Francisco: Harper and Row Publishers, Inc., 1984.

Gill, Sam. "Disenchantment." *Parabola* (Summer 1976):7-13

Bibliography

Harding, M. Esther. *The Value and Meaning of Depression.* New York: The Analytical Psychology Club of New York, Inc.

Hazleton, Lesley. *The Right To Feel Bad.* New York: Ballantine/Del Rey/Fawcett Books, 1985.

Hillman, James. "Betrayal" in *Loose Ends.* Dallas: Spring Publications, Inc., 1975.

Johnson, Robert. *We.* New York: Harper and Row Publishers, Inc., 1983.

Levinson, Daniel. *The Seasons of a Man's Life.* New York: Alfred A. Knopf, Inc., 1978.

Leech, Kenneth. *Experiencing God: Theology as Spirituality.* New York: Harper and Row Publishers, Inc., 1985.

May, Gerald G. *Addiction and Grace.* San Francisco: Harper and Row Publishers, Inc., 1988.

Meadow, Mary J. "The Dark Side of Mysticism: Depression and the 'dark night.' " *Pastoral Psychology* 33, (Winter 1984):104-125.

Tennov, Dorothy. *Love And Limerence: The Experience of Being In Love.* New York: Scarborough Books, 1980.

Van Kaam, Adrian. "Addiction: Counterfeit of Religious Experience." *Studies in Formative Spirituality* 7 (May 1987):243-245.

Viorst, Judith. *Necessary Losses.* New York: Simon and Schuster Inc., 1986.

Wetzel, Janice Wood. *Clinical Handbook of Depression.* Gardner Press Inc., 1984.